Top 25 locator map
(continues on inside
back cover)
◄───

# TwinPack
## Mallorca

**TONY KELLY**

Tony Kelly first visited Mallorca on a walking holiday in 1995 and he has been returning to the island ever since. In 2000 he was awarded a diploma by the Mallorca Tourist Board for his writing 'reflecting the true spirit and diverse nature of Mallorca'. An expert on Spain, his other guidebooks include *AA Essential Menorca*, *Essential Costa Brava* and *Spiral Gran Canaria*. He lives near Cambridge with his wife and young son.

If you have any comments or suggestions for this guide you can contact the editor at *Twinpacks@theAA.com*

**AA Publishing**
Find out more about AA Publishing and the wide range of services the AA provides by visiting our website at *www.theAA.com*

# Contents

# About this book

**TwinPack Mallorca** is divided into six sections to cover the six most important aspects of your visit to Mallorca. It includes:

- The author's view of the island and its people
- Suggested walks and excursions
- The top 25 sights to visit
- Features about different aspects of the island that make it special
- Detailed listings of restaurants, hotels, shops and nightlife
- Practical information

In addition, easy-to-read side panels provide fascinating extra facts and snippets, highlights of places to visit and invaluable practical advice.

## CROSS-REFERENCES

To help you make the most of your visit, cross-references, indicated by ➤, show you where to find additional information about a place or subject.

## MAPS

**The fold-out map** in the wallet at the back of the book is a large-scale island map of Mallorca.

**The Top 25 locator maps** found on the inside front and back covers of the book itself are for quick reference. They show the Top 25 Sights, described on pages 24–48, which are clearly plotted by number (**1**–**25**, not page number) in alphabetical order.

## PRICES

Where appropriate, an indication of the cost of an establishment is given by £ signs: £££ denotes higher prices, ££ denotes average prices, while £ denotes lower charges.

# MALLORCA
## life

# A Personal View

## MALLORCA OR MAJORCA?

Are they the same place or not? Yes and no. Majorca, with a hard 'J', is the paradise isle of the tour brochures, where the golden sand glistens beneath a clear blue sky and the nearest you get to local culture is a pastiche of a flamenco show. Mallorca, the local name for the island, is somewhere far more interesting and complex. This book is about Mallorca.

You probably think you know Mallorca already. It is, after all, Europe's favourite holiday island, visited by some 8 million tourists a year. Its popular image abroad is of high-rise concrete resorts overrun by British and German tourists, who spend all day on the beach and all evening in the bars, where the food and the beer taste exactly the same as at home.

Don't tell everybody, but Mallorca is just not like that. Yes, it has its ugly pockets, but these are easily avoided and most of the holiday resorts are a lot more restrained than you expect. The tourists are confined to a few crowded ghettoes on the coast while the rest of the island gets on with its life. Mallorca has mountains, pretty villages, monasteries, market towns, nature reserves, fishing ports and even one or two quiet beaches. And in its capital, Palma, it has one of the finest cities in Spain.

Of course, nowhere in Mallorca is untouched by tourism. Tourists have been visiting the island ever since Frédéric Chopin and George Sand spent the winter in Valldemossa in 1838. In an early sign of the tensions to come, Sand fell out with the locals over her foreign manners and morals. More than a century later, in the 1950s and 1960s, Mallorca was the birthplace of the Mediterranean package holiday and the islanders had to get used to everything from hippies to topless sunbathing. Fishing villages were destroyed to make way for soulless hotels, and unspoilt stretches of coastline were defaced by hastily built 'urbanisations'.

*Visitors to Cala Guya bask in the hot sun*

The island that led the way into mass tourism is now leading the way out. Mallorca has had enough of the so-called 'lager louts' who only want to get sunburnt and drunk as cheaply as possible. These days the island is developing a new image, as an upmarket destination for walking, golf and rural tourism. Cheap and cheerful is out, chic and cultured is in.

In truth, Mallorca has always appealed to a wide variety of visitors. The Spanish royal family spend their summer holidays here. Britain's Prince Charles is a frequent visitor, as was the late Princess Diana. Among the many foreign celebrities to have homes on the island are actor Michael Douglas, singer Annie Lennox, model Claudia Schiffer and racing driver Michael Schumacher. At the same time, Mallorca remains the favourite destination of millions of ordinary families, who know it as the best place in the Mediterranean for an old-fashioned seaside holiday.

Summer or winter, there is always something new to discover. You can walk in the mountains of the Serra de Tramuntana, where the air is scented with wild rosemary and pine. You can seek out chocolate-box villages, climb to hilltop castles, or explore the network of Roman roads which criss-crosses the central plain. Best of all, you can go where no guidebook leads you, leaving the coast far behind and venturing off the beaten track to discover those hidden towns and villages which are the essence of the authentic, timeless Mallorca.

### JOGGING ROUND MAJORCA

One of the earliest foreign visitors to Mallorca was the English writer Gordon West, whose book *Jogging Round Majorca*, published in 1929, captures the quaint charms of a largely rustic island. He wrote: 'Gazing down the steep, rock-strewn slopes…one dreads the inevitable day when the passing of some Lord Brougham will change the coast into a place of villas and casinos, of elaborate hotels and fashionable clothes.'

*The almond orchards of Andratx, with the Sierra de Tramuntana behind*

# Mallorca in Figures

**GEOGRAPHY**
- Mallorca is the largest of the Balearic Islands, a group that includes Menorca, Ibiza and Formentera.
- Mallorca measures 100km from east to west and 75km from north to south.
- Mallorca lies 200km south of Barcelona off the east coast of Spain.
- Mallorca has 555km of coastline and 80 beaches.
- Palma averages a daily maximum temperature of 21.4°C, and seven hours of sunshine per day throughout the year.

**PEOPLE**
- Of 630,000 people in Mallorca, half live in the capital Palma. The next biggest towns are Manacor (30,000) and Inca (22,000). The population has doubled since 1950 and includes a large number of expatriates – around 30,000 Germans and almost as many British.

**TOURISM**
- Mallorca received 1 million tourists in 1966, 3 million in 1978 and 8 million in 2000. In 2000, 41% of visitors were German, 26% were British and 12% were from mainland Spain.
- On busy days in summer up to 700 flights land at Palma airport, carrying up to 100,000 passengers.
- Mallorca has 200,000 hotel beds and 60,000 in tourist apartments.
- Mallorca has enough restaurant tables for a quarter of the population to eat out every night.
- Mallorca's GDP (Gross Domestic Product) per capita is more than 50% above the Spanish average. Two-thirds of the population work in tourism, which represents about 60% of GDP.

**LANGUAGE**
- The official languages are Catalan and Castilian Spanish; Catalan is now the preferred language in education and local government.
- Most people speak Mallorquín, a dialect of Catalan.

# People of Mallorca

## Ramón Llull

Ramón Llull (1235–1316) was a wealthy courtier in Palma until a disastrous seduction attempt led him to retire to Puig de Randa in isolation (► 41). Devoting himself to prayer and study, he wrote in Catalan and Latin on everything from algebra to metaphysics; he is widely seen as the father of the Catalan language. Recalled to the court by Jaume II, he established an Oriental language school at Valldemossa and learnt Arabic with the help of a Moorish slave. He was stoned to death attempting to convert Muslims in Tunisia.

## Junípero Serra

The Mallorcan missionary, Junípero Serra (1713–1784), is honoured in the Capitol in Washington, USA, as 'the founder of California'. Of course California was there already; but it was Serra, sent there at the age of 54 after 14 years in Mexico, who established the missions which grew into some of America's biggest cities, including San Diego and San Francisco. A museum in his home town of Petra (► 51) tells the story. He was beatified in 1988, the first step on the road to sainthood.

## Joan Miró

Though he was not strictly Mallorcan, Joan Miró (1893–1983), the Catalan artist, spent the last 27 years of his life in Mallorca and the islanders have adopted him as their own. His bright, surreal designs adorn everything from tourist posters (the widely used España and Mallorca logos are his) to T-shirts and the mural in the Parc de la Mar in Palma. His house and studio near Palma have been turned into a gallery of his work (► 31).

> **MICHAEL DOUGLAS (1944–)**
>
> The American actor Michael Douglas is a frequent visitor to Mallorca, where he has a home overlooking the north coast. His passion for Mallorca is reflected in his Costa Nord cultural centre (► 78) in Valldemossa. In 1999 he was awarded the silver siurell by the government of Mallorca for his role in promoting the island.

*Statue of Junípero Serra in Palma*

9

# A Chronology

| | |
|---|---|
| **5000 BC** | Evidence of human habitation in caves on the north coast. |
| **1300–800 BC** | The Talaiotic culture creates settlements like those at Artà and Capocorb Vell. |
| **400 BC** | First references to *honderos* (Balearic slingers) fighting in the Punic Wars. |
| **123 BC** | The island is conquered by the Romans, who name it Balearis Major, introduce vineyards and olives, and establish their capital at Pollentia, now Alcúdia. |
| **AD 426** | Vandal invasion and persecution of Christians. |
| **534** | Byzantine conquest restores Christianity and brings Mallorca into the province of Sardinia. |
| **902** | Arab invasion – Mallorca enters the Caliphate of Córdoba. Oranges and almonds are introduced, along with windmills and irrigation techniques. Palma, known as Medina Mayurqa, is the envy of Europe, with street lights and heated baths. |
| **1229** | The origins of modern Mallorca – conquest by Jaume I of Aragón. Catalan becomes main language. |
| **1275** | Ramón Llull establishes his first hermitage at Puig de Randa. |
| **1276** | On Jaume I's death, his kingdom is divided up and his son Jaume II becomes the first King of Mallorca. |
| **1276–1349** | The 'Golden Age of Independence' – the building of Castell de Bellver, Palau de l'Almudaina and Alcúdia's city walls. |
| **1349** | Jaume III is killed at Llucmajor and the island is reincorporated into Aragón. |
| **1492** | Modern Spain is created with the union of Aragón, Castile and Granada. |

| | |
|---|---|
| **16th–18th centuries** | Repeated pirate attacks lead to the building of watchtowers around the coast. |
| **1715** | After victory in the War of the Spanish Succession, Felipe V imposes central rule and the Castilian language. |
| **1836** | Steamer service opens between Mallorca and Spain. |
| **1879–1898** | Period of 'gold fever' due to the booming export trade in wine and almonds – until the vines are destroyed by the phylloxera virus, leading to mass emigration. |
| **1902–1903** | The Gran Hotel opens in Palma. Thomas Cook runs its first tours to Mallorca. |
| **1936–1939** | The Spanish Civil War, followed by dictatorship under General Franco. |
| **1950** | First charter flight lands in Mallorca. |
| **1960** | Son Sant Joan airport opened. |
| **1966** | Mallorca receives a million tourists. |
| **1975** | Death of Franco; restoration of the monarchy. |
| **1978** | A new constitution grants limited autonomy to the Spanish regions. |
| **1983** | The Balearic Islands become an autonomous region with their capital at Palma. Catalan becomes the official language. |
| **1986** | Spain joins the European Community. |
| **1988** | A new coastal law prohibits further development within 100m of the sea. |
| **1997** | New terminal at Son Sant Joan airport increases capacity to 27 million passengers a year. |
| **2002** | Euro banknotes and coins are introduced across Spain. |

# Best of Mallorca

*Take the tram to Port de Sóller and the boat to Sa Calobra*

If you only have a short time to visit Mallorca, and are looking for the best way to experience the essence of the island, here are some suggestions for activities and places that shouldn't be missed:

- Spend a day in Palma exploring the old city, then join the evening *passeig* along the waterfront for a drink in one of the island's trendiest bars (➤ 34–38).

- Take the joyride to Sóller on a vintage electric train through the mountains (➤ 46; also ➤ 16).

- Take a boat trip around the coast, and enjoy the view as you pass hidden coves which you cannot reach in a car.

- Walk in the Serra de Tramuntana (➤ 44), breathing in the heady mix of fresh air, sea breeze and scented wild herbs.

- Sit at a quayside restaurant eating fresh fish – choose from any one of the island's ports (➤ 62–69).

- Visit the monastery at Valldemossa where Frédéric Chopin and George Sand spent the winter of 1838–1839 (➤ 48).

- Drive (or walk) to a hilltop sanctuary to experience 'the other Mallorca' – if you want to get away from it all, stay the night.

- Visit the traditional market at Sineu (➤ 45) to haggle over everything from sausages to sheep.

- Get a tan on a crowded beach – you haven't 'done' Mallorca until you have, but remember your sunscreen.

- Find out where there is a local festival going on (➤ 22) – and drop everything to get there.

# MALLORCA
## how to organise your time

# A Walk Around Palma

## INFORMATION

**Distance** 3.5km
**Time** 2 hours plus coffee, browsing, visits – allow half a day
**Start/end point** Plaça d'Espanya
🏛 Fundació la Caixa (££)
✉ Plaça Weyler 3

This walk starts in Plaça d'Espanya and passes close to all of Palma's main sights. Begin by heading for Mercat Olivar (► 74), where you can look round the market. Leave via Plaça Olivar and turn left into Carrer Sant Miquel.

Soon you reach Plaça Major with its outdoor cafés and street entertainers. Continue across the square; fork right into Carrer Jaume II.

At the end of this pedestrian shopping street, don't fail to look up at the *modernista* façade of Sa Nostra bank before turning left into Plaça Cort. Beyond a gnarled olive tree you see the town hall. Take the short street to the left of the town hall to reach Plaça Santa Eulàlia; cross this square diagonally and take Carrer Morey.

*Plaça Major – a good place to stop for a coffee. There is a craft market held here on summer mornings*

This brings you into the heart of the old city. Take your time here admiring the courtyards; make sure you don't miss Casa Oleza at No 9. Continue straight on to Carrer Miramar and turn right onto the city walls.

The cathedral (► 37) is above you; in order to visit it and the palace, climb the steps up to a large wooden cross. Once back on the walls, continue until you drop to the S'Hort del Rei gardens (► 38). Cross Plaça Reina and walk up the Born, turning right by Bar Bosch into Carrer Unió.

Look out for the old Gran Hotel (► 36) on your left and the bakery opposite, two good examples of *modernista* style. Beyond the theatre, the road bends left and becomes La Rambla; stroll up this promenade among the flower stalls. At the top of La Rambla, turn right into Carrer Oms and follow it back to Plaça d'Espanya.

# A Drive Across the Central Plain

This lovely drive criss-crosses the central plain, following old Roman roads through almond and apricot groves on its way to several small market towns. Start in Petra, following signs to Santa Margalida from the parish church. Bypass Santa Margalida by bearing left towards Muro. In Muro (▶ 51), Carrer Major takes you to the museum – well worth a visit.

Continue along Carrer Major, over a crossroads and past the church of Sant Joan Baptista towards Sa Pobla. Next you cross a fertile land of windmills, red earth and potato fields. Up ahead you see the mountains.

From Sa Pobla, follow signs to Llubi; when you reach Llubi go uphill into the village and down again to reach a main road, where you turn left and immediately right towards Sineu (▶ 45). Drystone walls to either side line the route. As you approach Sineu, turn left at the crossroads (signposted to Sant Joan) to pass underneath a modern sculpture outside the S'Estació art gallery.

Continue towards Sant Joan. Before reaching the village, turn right and travel toward Montuïri. Bypassing Montuïri, cross the Palma–Manacor highway by the Orquídea pearl shop and head for Porreres. A short detour takes you up to the Santuari de Montesió. Leave Porreres in the direction of Vilafranca de Bonany. Turn left in Vilafranca and pass Els Calderers on your right.

You could visit the stately home of Els Calderers, taking a short cut to Sant Joan. Take the next right turn to Sant Joan, from where you can return to Petra (▶ 51). There are excellent views as you approach.

## INFORMATION

**Distance** 81km
**Time** 3 hours
**Start/end point** Petra
🚻 Centre (£)
✉ Avinguda Bisbe Campins, Porreres

*The reclaimed marshland of Sa Pobla has proved ideal for agriculture*

# A Day Out by Train and Tram

The opening of a railway line from Palma to Sóller in 1912, and a tram linking Sóller to its port the following year, brought the northwest coast within easy reach of the capital. The vintage carriages are still in use, providing a joyride for tourists and a relief for locals from the terrors of the Palma–Sóller road. Five trains a day leave from Plaça d'Espanya in Palma – the 10:40 is labelled the *turistico* but all you get for the extra cost is a more crowded train and a short photo stop.

## INFORMATION

**Time** 1.5 hours each way
**Start point** Plaça d'Espanya
📧 Most city/island-wide buses terminate here
**End point** Port de Sóller
🍴 Tapas bars (£)
✉ Plaça Constitució, Sóller

The train, all mahogany panels and brass fittings, leaves Palma amid a bustle of hisses, hoots and whistles before rattling down the city streets and into the suburbs. Soon you are out on the plain, passing small country stations and pigs rooting beneath the trees. You can get off at Bunyola and climb up the hill to reach the centre of this sleepy village, with cafés on the main square.

*Take the miniature train from Palma to Sóller*

Stay on the train and soon you start to climb, entering a 3km tunnel before returning to daylight for the drop, through a dizzying series of bends, to Sóller (► 46).

The 'Orange Express' tram to Port de Sóller runs hourly, connecting with the arrival of the train. Stand on the platform as it clatters through orchards and back gardens and you can imagine you are living 50 years earlier. The 5km journey to the port takes 20 minutes.

If you do not want to return the same way, buses leave from the jetty for Palma via Deià and Valldemossa.

# A Walk from Santa Eugènia

This simple walk gives spectacular views for the minimum of effort. Leave the village of Santa Eugènia and head in the direction of Santa Maria del Camí. After 1km turn left to Ses Coves along a narrow lane which bends left, then descends and you see Ses Coves ('the caves') used at various times as pirate hideaways and wine cellars. One cave contains an ancient wine-press. When the road divides, fork left; soon you reach some iron gates at the entrance to a track on your right.

*Selling olives at Santa Maria del Camí market*

Here you have an optional detour to the summit of Puig d'En Marron, adding an hour to your walk. Step over the low wall besides the gates and climb until the road runs out. Continue along a mud track through the pine woods, keeping right at each fork, until you emerge onto a wide open plateau. Return to the iron gates by the same route and turn right to rejoin the main walk.

Follow the lane briefly uphill; when the lane divides, take the track on the left. After passing an arched entrance to a well, turn immediately left through an orchard towards a house.

To the right of the house, the wall is marked with a red dot; climb from here to a pass. Here you can clamber over a stone wall to your left to reach the cross on the summit of Puig de Santa Eugènia. This is the high point of the walk, with wonderful views that stretch across the plain to the mountains in the distance. On the opposite clifftop is one of Mallorca's oddest sights – the cockpit of a broken-up plane.

Retrace your steps to the stone wall and then follow the path that leads through the bushes on your left to return to Santa Eugènia.

## INFORMATION

**Distance** 4.5km (optional detour adds 3km)

**Time** 1–2 hours

**Start/end point** Santa Eugènia

🚌 From Palma – only one or two buses per day, so check timetable

🍴 Ca Na Cantona (£)

✉ Carrer Balenguera, Santa Eugènia

☎ 971 144031

1

# A Drive in the West

This drive gives an excellent introduction to the mountain and coastal scenery of western Mallorca.

## INFORMATION

**Distance** 62km
**Time** 3 hours plus lunch and time at La Granja
**Start/end point** Andratx
🏠 La Granja (£)
✉ 971 610032

Start in Andratx, taking the C710 to Estellencs about halfway up the main street. Immediately the road begins to climb through pine woods and tunnels, with occasional glimpses of the sea. Follow this beautiful twisting coast road to the village of Estellencs, one of the prettiest in Mallorca, with its ochre-coloured houses, narrow, steep cobbled streets and women doing their washing at the village well. After another 5km, stop at the Mirador de Ses Animes and clamber up to the 16th-century watchtower for views right along the northwest coast. Soon after this you reach Banyalbufar (► 58), with its spectacular terracing.

When the C710 turns off left towards Valldemossa, keep straight on the PM110, signposted to Palma. After 1km you see a sign to La Granja on your right. You could easily spend 2–3 hours at this display of Mallorcan traditions (► 32).

Leaving La Granja, take the narrow road to Puigpunyent from the car park. Follow this road for 10km, a dramatic journey through olive groves in

*You pass several coastal watchtowers, including this one near the village of Estellencs*

the shadow of Puig de Galatzó. The road continues through Puigpunyent and on to Galilea (► 50), a mountain village with a couple of tapas bars and views out to sea. From here the road twists and turns down to the village of Es Capdella. Turn right in the village and follow signs back to Andratx.

# The Archduke's Bridlepath Walk

This walk was mapped out by Archduke Ludwig Salvator during tours of his estates by mule; as well as spectacular coastal views, it gives an introduction to traditional mountain industries. You pass *sitjas* (round charcoal ovens), *casas de neu* (snow pits where winter snows were stored beneath a layer of ash), *forns de calç* (lime kilns) and *caças a coll* (thrush nets slung between the trees). The route is for experienced walkers only. Take food and water, a map, compass and whistle and protection from sun, wind and rain. The weather on the mountains can change very quickly.

## INFORMATION

**Distance** 13km
**Time** 6 hours
**Start/end point** Valldemossa
🚌 From Palma, Deià or Port de Sóller
🍴 Take a picnic

Begin at the car park opposite Bar Sa Mata on the road through Valldemossa. Climb the hill behind the car park towards the cemetery. Take the second right (Carrer Joan Fuster), then first left (Carrer de les Oliveres), continuing onto a rough track when the road runs out. You climb gently at first, towards a group of pines, then more steeply, following red waymarks to a clearing. From here it is a short, tough climb to a mirador and the start of the Camí de S'Arxiduc, marked by a ruined stone refuge.

Follow the waymarks onto a high plateau and continue for about two hours. For the best views of all, a one-hour diversion (just as the main path bears round to the right for its descent) takes you to the summit of the Teix, from where most of Mallorca is visible on a clear day. The path drops back down to Valldemossa through a wooded valley, passing a shelter where you can camp in summer.

For a shorter walk to the foot of the Teix, you can simply do the final section in reverse. Leave Valldemossa by walking past Son Gual, the large old house with a tower seen just above the main road as you enter Palma (the path is signposted 'Teix-Refugi'). The climb through the valley to the shelter and back will take a couple of hours if you walk briskly.

*There are splendid views of the coastline from the Archduke's estates*

19

# Finding Peace & Quiet

**RIGHTS OF WAY**

Walkers have the right of way on all coastal paths, plus routes to miradors, monasteries and mountain peaks (except Puig Major). In recent years, many landowners have attempted to deny access by erecting 'private' signs. If challenged, just state clearly where you are going.

*Almond trees near Andratx – it is still surprisingly easy to get away from it all in Mallorca*

If you want peace and quiet in Mallorca, go in winter – only 10 per cent of foreign tourists visit between November and March. The island is particularly beautiful in February, when almond blossom carpets the ground like snow. Even in the height of summer, there are plenty of opportunities to escape the crowds. Half of the locals live in Palma, and 90 per cent of the tourists stay on a few small stretches of coast – which leaves large areas of Mallorca just waiting to be explored.

## WALKING

The obvious areas are the mountains, especially the Serra de Tramuntana (▶ 44). At the lower levels, up to around 700m, you walk through *garrigue*, a typical Mediterranean landscape where Aleppo pines mix with wild olives and the stony ground sprouts beautiful wild flowers – orchids and peonies and cistus and asphodel – in spring. (Spring here arrives early, from late February through to May.) Higher up, you reach the *maquis* scrubland, where little grows apart from thorny bushes of heather, bracken, rosemary and broom. Above 1,000m the land is barren – but the views from this height are magnificent and the sense of isolation complete.

Take sensible precautions when walking in the mountains – good boots, extra clothing, food and water, a map, compass and whistle. If you prefer more gentle walks, just strike out along any of the minor roads between the small towns on the plain, or follow a coastal footpath to find your own private bay.

## BIRDS

Mallorca is a paradise for birdwatchers, who come from all over Europe each spring and autumn to see migrating birds on their way to and from wintering in Africa. The best times are April to May and September to October, and the best areas are S'Albufera (► 42) and the Salines de Llevant near Ses Salines. The reedbeds of S'Albufera come alive each spring with the song of herons and warblers; other species include egrets, terns, hoopoes, sandpipers and woodcat shrike. Numerous wading birds and wildfowl are attracted to the salt marshes at Ses Salines, including plovers, stilts, water rails and black-tailed godwits. Good spots for watching seabirds include Cap de Ses Salines on the south coast and Cap de Formentor in the northeast (► 27), where shags and shearwaters nestle on the cliffs.

*The wetlands of S'Albufera are a protected reserve*

**BIRDS OF PREY**

The mountains of the Serra de Tramuntana are a haven for birds of prey, including ospreys, peregrines, Montagu's harriers and Eleanora's falcons. Rarest of all are the black vultures, of which only a few dozen remain in the area around Lluc monastery. An exhibition at the monastery describes a conservation programme to protect both these and another endangered species, the Mallorcan midwife toad. The best places to see black vultures, and other predatory birds, are at the Cúber and Gorg Blau reservoirs on the road through the mountains from Lluc to Sóller.

21

# What's On

**JANUARY**
*Cabalgata de los Reyes Magos* (5 Jan): The Three Kings arrive by boat in Palma to distribute gifts to the city's children.
*Sant Antoni Abat* (16–17 Jan): Processions of pets and farm animals: Palma, Artà, Sa Pobla.
*Sant Sebastià* (19 Jan): Bonfires and barbecues in Palma's squares.

**FEBRUARY**
*Sa Rúa* (final weekend before Lent): Carnival in Palma and elsewhere with bonfires, fancy dress and processions of decorated floats. In Montuïri the Carnival is known as *Darres Dies* (Last Days).

**MARCH/APRIL**
*Semana Santa* (Holy Week): Easter preparation begins on Palm Sunday, with the blessing of palm and olive branches. During Holy Week the biggest Palma procession is on Maundy Thursday. On the evening of Good Friday a figure of Christ is lowered from his cross in Pollença and carried down the Calvary steps in silence. A similar event takes place in Felanitx.

**MAY**
*Moros i Cristians* (8–10 May): Mock battles between heroes and infidels in Sóller, commemorating 1561 when local women helped to defeat a band of Turkish pirates.

**JUNE**
*Sant Pere* (28–29 Jun): Processions of boats in Palma, Port d'Andratx and Port d'Alcúdia in honour of the patron saint of fishermen.

**JULY**
*La Verge del Carme* (16 Jul): Boat processions in ports including Cala Rajada, Port de Pollença and Port de Sóller.
*Santa Catalina Thomás* (27–28 Jul): Homage to Mallorca's patron saint in Valldemossa.

**AUGUST**
*Sant Bartomeu* (24 Aug): Devil-dancing in Montuïri at one of Mallorca's oldest festivals.
*Sant Agusti* (28 Aug): *Cavallets* dances in Felanitx, with children dressed up as cardboard horses being chased by giants to the accompaniment of bagpipes, flutes and drums.

**SEPTEMBER/OCTOBER**
Harvest festivals including a melon festival in Vilafranca de Bonany (second Sun in Sep), a wine fair in Binissalem (last Sun in Sep), and a *botifarró* (blood sausage) festival in Sant Joan (third Sun in Oct).

**DECEMBER**
*Festa de l'Estendard* (31 Dec): Anniversary of the Christian conquest; procession from Palma's town hall to Mass at the cathedral.

# MALLORCA's
## top 25 sights

The sights are shown on the maps on the inside front cover and inside back cover, numbered **1**–**25** alphabetically

23

# Alcúdia

## INFORMATION

🔁 D1
🚌 From Palma/Port
d'Alcúdia
❓ Market held Tue & Sun

**Ciutat Romà**
🕐 Tue–Fri 10–1:15,
3:30–5:15, Sat–Sun
10–1:15
💶 Cheap

**Museu Monogràfic de
Pollentia**
✉ Carrer Sant Jaume 30
☎ 971 547004
🕐 Tue–Fri 10–1:30,
3:30–5:30, Sat–Sun
10:30–1
💶 Cheap

**This is a gem of a place. It is a perfectly restored walled city on the site of a Roman settlement, with remains of Roman houses and an amphitheatre. You see a maze of narrow streets enclosed by medieval ramparts, presented as a model of Mallorca's new tourist image.**

There were Phoenician and Greek settlements, but Alcúdia's heyday was in the 2nd century BC, when as Pollentia ('power') it was the capital of Roman Mallorca. Destroyed in the 6th century by Vandals, the town returned to greatness under the Moors, who built *al-kudia* ('the town on the hill'). The existing walls were added after the Spanish conquest in the 14th century.

You enter the city through one of the two town gates – the Portal del Moll, with two square towers and two massive palm trees standing guard, is the symbol of Alcúdia. The narrow streets of the old town, especially Carrer d'en Serra, are redolent of Palma's Arab quarter.

*Portal del Moll, once the gateway to Alcúdia from its port, leads directly into the heart of the city*

A short walk from the parish church of Sant Jaume takes you to three interesting sights, connected by signposted footpaths. Closest are the remains of Roman houses at Pollentia, **Ciutat Romà**; near here are the well-preserved Teatre Romà (Roman amphitheatre), and Oratori de Santa Anna, one of the islands's oldest churches. Explore the Roman remains, then interpret them at the **Museu Monogràfic de Pollentia**.

## Artà

**Derived from the Arabic word *jertan* ('garden'), Artà has been occupied for at least 3,000 years, as evidenced by the Bronze Age site at Ses Païsses, just outside the town. Nowadays Artà is a prosperous little town near the coast, which gets particularly lively each Tuesday on market day.**

From the parish church of Transfiguració del Senyor, an avenue of cypress trees leads to Artà's crowning glory, its hilltop fortress and Santuari de Sant Salvador. The view down over the rooftops, a jumble of tiles in every shade of brown, is one of the sights of Mallorca. On the site of a Moorish fortress, the original sanctuary walls and chapel were rebuilt in the 19th century. Walk around the battlements, rest in a courtyard, then look into the church with its vivid paintings of two Mallorcan heroes – Jaume the Conqueror receiving the surrender of the *walis*, and Ramón Llull being stoned to death in Tunisia. There is also a painting of Sant Antoni, patron saint of Artà and of animals, seen as always with a small pig. Each January the saint is commemorated with a masked procession and a blessing of pets. Artà's big festival, Sant Antoni de Juny, dates back to 1581 and features dancers with cardboard horses strapped to their hips.

Artà's small **museum**, housed inside Sa Nostra bank, has archaeological discoveries from Greek and Roman periods.

**INFORMATION**

➕ E2
🚌 From Palma and Cala Rajada
🎫 Market held Tue; Sant Antoni Abat, procession and blessing of pets, 16–17 Jan; Sant Antoni de Juny, *cavallets* horse dances, 13 Jun

**Museum**
✉️ Carrer Estrella 4
☎️ 971 835017
🕐 Mon–Fri 10–1
💰 Cheap

*A flight of steps leads to Artà's hilltop sanctuary*

# Badia de Palma (Palma Bay)

## INFORMATION

➕ B3

🍴 Numerous bars and
restaurants in all the
resorts (£)

🚌 From Palma to all the
resorts

🚢 Boat tours of Palma Bay
in summer from Palma,
S'Arenal, Palma Nova and
Magaluf

♿ Level beach promenades
at Platja de Palma and
Magaluf

↔ Castell de Bellver (➤ 35)

**The good, the bad and the ugly sides of Mallorca's tourist development meet along this 25km stretch of coast. Like it or loathe it, you are bound to spend some time in Palma Bay.**

The former villages of S'Arenal and Magaluf sit facing each other across Palma Bay. Once, a fisherman casting his net at S'Arenal could have gazed around an empty coastline where the only prominent buildings would have been Palma's cathedral and castle. Nowadays he would barely be able to distinguish them among a continuous stretch of hotels, a concrete jungle extending all the way to Magaluf. And he wouldn't be there anyway as there are few fish left to catch.

Even if you are not staying here, you should visit at least once to see some of the best, and the worst, that Mallorca has to offer. Each of the resorts has its own character – young or old, British or German, cheap-and-cheerful or jet-set rich. One moment you can be in Portals Nous, its marina crammed with millionaires' yachts (you have to be seriously rich just to look at the restaurant menus), the next in seedy Magaluf, all British pubs and wet T-shirt contests.

Occasionally you come across a glimpse of what this coastline must have been like. Follow the road beyond Magaluf through the pine woods. Suddenly you are among tiny coves where, out of season, you might still find your own private beach. Eventually you reach the headland of Cap de Cala Figuera (➤ 50) where you can look back at sweeping views of the bay. Cliffs plunge into the clear blue sea, with not a hotel in sight. Come up here at midnight for utter peace and solitude; even so, if you listen carefully you might just be able to hear the disco beat of Magaluf pounding away beneath you.

## Cap de Formentor

**This wild peninsula on Mallorca's northeast tip has stunning views, sandy beaches and the island's original luxury hotel. Hotel Formentor has been pampering the rich and famous ever since it opened in 1929.**

### INFORMATION

🔲 E1

🍴 Café with snacks at Cap de Formentor (£); restaurant (£££) in Hotel Formentor

🚌 From Palma and Port de Pollença in summer

⛴ From Port de Pollença to Formentor beach and Cap de Formentor in summer

❓ The best time to see birds and flowers is spring

The 20km drive from Port de Pollença to Mallorca's most northerly point has dramatic scenery. Cliffs 400m tall jut into the sea, their weird rock formations attracting nesting seabirds, while pine trees seem to grow out of the rocks. The drive is famously scary – local legend has it that the parish priest and bus driver arrived at the Pearly Gates, and only the driver was admitted. The reason? He had led far more people to pray.

Six kilometres from Port de Pollença you reach the Mirador des Colomer – scramble up the steps for views over a rocky islet. A path opposite leads to an old watchtower from which you can see the whole of the peninsula as well as the bays of Pollença and Alcúdia. The road continues through pine woods and past more *miradors* (each one indicated with a picture of a camera) before tunnelling through En Fumat mountain, where you look down over Mallorca's most inaccessible beach. Eventually you reach a lighthouse with the inevitable bar and shop, with views all the way to Menorca on a good day.

On the way back, stop at Formentor beach and the Hotel Formentor. The fine sandy beach used to be reserved for the hotel's guests, but democracy has opened it to the masses.

*Walkers on the path to the viewpoint at Mirador des Colomar*

# Castell d'Alaró

## INFORMATION

✚ C2

☎ Sanctuary: 971 510480

◑ Open access

🍴 Es Verger (££) on the way
up; simple restaurant (££)
at the sanctuary

🚌 From Palma to Alaró

↔ Orient (► 51)

**A popular walk, ending with a steep climb, to a ruined castle and hilltop chapel offering spectacular views all the way to the sea.**

A castle has stood on this site since Moorish times; it was so impregnable that the Arab commander was able to hold out for two years after the Christian conquest. Later, in 1285, two heroes of Mallorcan independence, Cabrit and Brassa, defended the castle against Alfonsó III of Aragón and were burned alive on a spit when he finally took it by storm. Their punishment was a consequence of their impudent defiance of the king. They pretended to confuse Alfonsó's name with that of a local fish – *anfós*, shouting: 'We like our *anfós* grilled.' The present ruins date from the 15th century and seem almost to grow out of the rock, dominating the landscape for miles around.

The climb up here is one of Mallorca's most popular walks, especially on Sundays. From the town of Alaró it is a stiff climb of about two hours, following the signs from the PM210 to Orient; you can also leave from Orient (► 51), following a small path opposite L'Hermitage hotel, again taking around two hours in total. The paths converge above Es Verger restaurant (you can even bring a car this far if you don't mind the potholes and the hairpin bends), where you can fill up with roast lamb to fortify you for the final steep section.

*The view from inside the ruins at Castell d'Alaró*

At last you reach the castle, 800m above sea level; look back at the view, stretching across the entire plain to Palma and out to sea. A few minutes further brings you to the summit, with a small chapel and sanctuary, and (bliss!) a restaurant and bar. You can stay the night here in one of the simple rooms.

# Coves d'Artà

**A fascinating network of underground caverns, whose weird stalactites and stalagmites conjure up mysterious images of Heaven and Hell.**

If you only have time to visit one set of caves on the east coast, this is the one to see. Now that they are a sanitised tourist attraction, it is hard to imagine how French geologist Édouard Martel felt when he first stepped into these caves, dark, mysterious and terrifying, in 1876. In fact they had been known about for centuries – Jaume I found 2,000 Arabs hiding here with their cattle during the Christian conquest and they were later used by hermits, pirates and smugglers – but it was Martel who first studied and chronicled these grottoes, 46m above the sea at Cap Vermell, at the instigation of Archduke Ludwig Salvator. Another early visitor was Jules Verne; the caves are said to have inspired his *Journey to the Centre of the Earth*.

The guided tour comes with special effects and the various chambers are given Dantesque names – Hell, Purgatory, Paradise. The descent into Hell is swiftly followed by a *son et lumière* display. Stalactites point down from the mouldy roof like daggers, somehow defying gravity. One of the chambers is as large as the nave of Palma cathedral, and the Queen of Pillars, a stalagmite 22m tall, could almost be a Gothic column. It is growing upwards at the rate of 2cm every 100 years; in another 5,000 years or so it will be joined to the ceiling.

You emerge from the caves to a view of the sea, framed by the cavern entrance. Disabled visitors and others with limited mobility will find the staircases in here particularly difficult. All visitors should be sensibly shod, as the floor can be slippery.

## INFORMATION

🔲 F2
☎ 971 841293
🕐 Jul–Sep, daily 10–7; Oct–Jun, daily 10–5
🍴 Bars at Platja de Canyamel near by (£)
🚍 From Artà and Cala Rajada in summer
♿ None
💶 Moderate
🔗 Artá (➤ 25)

*Artificial lighting results in some spectacular colours in the caves*

## Deià

**INFORMATION**

➕ B2

🍽 Wide choice of restaurants and bars (£–£££)

🚌 From Palma, Valldemossa and Port de Sóller

🔄 Son Marroig (➤ 47)

❓ Classical music festival, Aug–Sep

**This idyllic village of green-shuttered, ochre-coloured houses has become a millionaires' hideaway in the shadow of the Teix mountain.**

Deià could have been just another pretty Mallorcan village had Robert Graves not decided to make it his home. The English poet and novelist first moved here in 1932 with his mistress Laura Riding and returned in 1946 with his second wife. Muses followed, friends came to stay, and before long Deià had established a reputation as a foreign artists' colony. Now it is on every tourist itinerary as the prime example of 'the other Mallorca', and this small village contains two luxury hotels. Rich foreign residents, like the actor Michael Douglas, are

*Cars parked in the main square at Deià, popular with artists*

apt to bemoan the arrival of tour buses; the few locals who remain are philosophical about outsiders.

Graves was hardly the first to discover Deià. An 1878 guidebook noted its 'collection of strange and eccentric foreigners' and it has stayed that way ever since. Climb the Carrer es Puig, Deià's only real street, passing ceramic Stations of the Cross, to reach the parish church and the small cemetery where Graves is buried. His tombstone, like many others, is inscribed in simple handwriting set into the drying concrete – Robert Graves, Poeta, 1895–1985. If you want to know more, read *Wild Olives – Life in Majorca with Robert Graves* by his son William Graves.

From Deià you can scramble down to Cala de Deià, a small shingle beach set in an attractive cove, where local artists still continue the Graves tradition of naked swimming and long parties at weekends.

# Fundació Pilar i Joan Miró

**Joan Miró's house and studio were built on a hillside to capitalise on the special quality of the Mallorcan light, which was so important to him.**

The painter and sculptor Joan Miró spent most of his life in Barcelona, but both his wife and mother were Mallorcan and he always longed to return to the scene of his childhood holidays to draw inspiration from what he called 'the light of Mallorca'. In 1956, aged 63, he bought a house and studio in Cala Major. He lived here until he died in 1983, after which the building was enlarged to hold a permanent exhibition of his works. Changing displays of Miró's work are shown in galleries of bleached stone.

The collection includes more than 100 paintings, 25 sculptures and 3,000 studio pieces but only a small amount is displayed at any one time. The paintings are almost childish, all vivid splashes of bright primary colours, influenced by his love of peasant traditions and his fascination with *siurells* (clay whistles). Anyone tempted to remark that their child could do better should take a look at the heavily realistic work that Miró was producing aged eight – the fantasy came later. Works on display include the draft for UNESCO's *Mural del Sol* in Paris.

Glance into Miró's studio, left untouched since his death, with work in progress, open tins of paint and black stains all over the floor.

## INFORMATION

🔳 B2

✉ Carrer Joan de Saridakis 29, Cala Major

☎ 971 701420

🕐 15 May–15 Sep, Tue–Sat 10–7, Sun 10–3; 16 Sep–14 May, Tue–Sat 10–6, Sun 10–3

🍴 Café (£)

🚌 4 from Palma

♿ Good

🎫 Moderate

*A sculpture by Joan Miró in the grounds of his former studio*

31

# La Granja

## INFORMATION

🔷 B2
☎ 971 610032
🕐 Apr–Sep, daily 10–7;
   Oct–Mar, daily 10–6
🍴 Restaurant (£)
🚌 From Palma
♿ None
💷 Expensive
🔄 Banyalbufar (► 58)
❓ Folk fiesta, Wed, Fri 3–5

**This grand house, standing on a site occupied since Moorish times, was once a Cistercian monastery, and now provides a fascinating insight into Mallorcan life in earlier days.**

This country house, just south of Banyalbufar, is on a site known since Roman times for its natural spring. When Jaume I conquered Mallorca he divided the island into four feudal estates, giving one to Count Nuno Sanç, who settled at La Granja. In 1239 the Count handed the estate to Cistercian monks to found Mallorca's first monastery. Since 1447 it has been a private house owned by various noble families; most of what you see today dates from the 17th century.

Highlights of the tour include an aristocratic drawing-room with its own theatre, the family chapel and a dungeon with a torture chamber – but the real reason for visiting La Granja is to learn about rural Mallorcan traditions. Workshops, cellars and kitchens contain displays of everyday objects. And on Wednesday and Friday afternoons, women in traditional costume give demonstrations of lace-making, embroidery and spinning, donkeys turn threshing-wheels and there are tastings of cheese, wine, sausages, doughnuts and fig cake. Escape from the tour groups by walking in the grounds, which contain botanical gardens, waterfalls and a thousand-year-old yew – there is a 1,200m signed walk. And look out for the exhibit listed in the guide as 'dog' – it is just that, a *ca de bestair*, or black-coated Mallorcan guard dog on a chain.

If you have not gorged yourself on free samples during the course of your visit, the restaurant serves good Mallorcan staple dishes like *pa amb oli* and *sopes mallorquines*.

## Lluc

**This is Mallorca's most sacred site – a former monastery in a spectacular setting in the Serra de Tramuntana, housing a much-venerated ancient wooden statue of the Virgin.**

Lluc has been a centre of pilgrimage since the 13th century when an Arab shepherd boy, newly converted to Christianity, discovered a dark wooden statue of the Virgin in a cleft in the rock. The image was placed in the local church but three times it returned miraculously to its cave, whereupon the villagers recognised a message from God and built a chapel to house it.

*La Moreneta* ('the Little Dark One') is now encrusted with precious stones, and sits in a chapel decorated with the arms of every Mallorcan town. Pilgrims and tourists queue to pay homage, especially on Sundays and at 11AM before the daily concerts by Els Blauets choir. The choir, named after their blue cassocks, was established in 1531, comprising 40 boys, 'natives of Mallorca, of pure blood, sound in grammar and song'. The service is marred by the whirring and flashing of cameras, and if it's meditation you seek, come back instead for the evening Mass.

The monastery complex includes Els Porxerets, the former pilgrims' quarters with stabling beneath the rooms, and the Way of the Rosary, with touches by Antoni Gaudí. From the hilltop cross you look down over a farmland valley and up into the pine-covered mountains. You can stay at Lluc but it is more like a hotel than a hermitage – the 100 'cells' have en suite bathrooms and there are restaurants and bars. There is also a museum – in addition to the displays of ceramics, chalices and coins there is a collection of paintings by the 20th-century Mallorcan artist Josep Coll Bardolet.

### INFORMATION

- C1
- 971 871525
- Museum: daily 10–5:30; Monastery: daily 9–8:30
- Sa Fonda (££) in the former monks' refectory
- Two buses daily from Palma and Inca
- Monastery: free. Museum: cheap
- Sa Calobra (► 43), Serra de Tramuntana (► 44)
- Choir concert daily 11:15 followed by Mass at 11:30; second service at dusk open to those staying overnight; annual night-time pilgrimage from Palma to Lluc on foot (48km) – usually held in first week of Aug

# Palma

## INFORMATION

➕ B2

ℹ️ Carrer de Sant
   Domingo 11,
   Palma 07001
   ☎ 971 724090;
   Parc de les Estacions,
   Palma 07002
   ☎ 971 754329

🍴 Wide range of cafés and
   restaurants (£–£££)

❓ Festivals throughout the
   year, including daily
   processions during Holy
   Week and fishing boat
   procession (Festival of
   Sant Pere) in June

**Palma comes as a surprise to many people: stylish, sophisticated, intimate yet bursting with life. Half of Mallorca's population live here, enjoying the island's best restaurants and shops as well as a thriving arts scene.**

Known to the Arabs as Medina Mayurqa and to Mallorcans simply as *Ciutat* (City), Palma is named after the Roman city of Palmaria. Here you can uncover the different layers of Mallorcan history. The Roman city still exists, a metre or two beneath the ground; Roman remains are still discovered near the cathedral, itself built on the site of a mosque that was once a Roman temple. The royal palace replaced an Arab *alcázar*.

The city you see today, however, is a relatively recent creation. The tree-lined promenades of La Rambla and Passeig des Born, home to florists and newspaper sellers, were built in the 19th century on a dried-up river bed. The walls which once surrounded the city were pulled down to create the ring road Las Avingudas, and Passeig Marítim, the waterfront highway and promenade, was only reclaimed from the sea in the 1950s.

Most of the main sights are located within the area bounded by the old walls, especially to the north and east of the cathedral. Wander along any alley in the ancient Arab quarter, peering through wrought-iron gates and heavy wooden doors, and you will be rewarded with glimpses of one magnificent patio after another, with their stone staircases, galleries and arcades.

But you have not truly seen Palma until you have surveyed it from the waterfront, with the cathedral and Almudaina palace rising proudly above the defensive walls of the old city, their golden sandstone lit up by the afternoon sun.

# Palma's Castell de Bellver

**A well-preserved 14th-century royal fortress with fragrant pine woods, an interesting museum and superb views over Palma Bay. Castell de Bellver is unique among Spanish castles in being entirely round.**

**INFORMATION**

➕ B2
✉ Parc Bellver
☎ 971 730657
🕐 Apr–Sep, Mon–Sat 8AM–8:30PM; Oct–Mar, Mon–Sat 8–7:15
🚌 3 or 21 to Plaça Gomila
💶 Cheap; free on Sun, when museum closed

Looking up at this castle, so perfectly maintained, it is hard to believe that it has been standing for almost 700 years. It was begun by Jaume II in 1300 and built by Pere Salvà, architect of the Almudaina Palace. Three large towers surround a central courtyard, connected by an arch to a free-standing keep. The courtyard itself is on two levels, the ground floor with semicircular arches and a flat roof, the upper level with Gothic arches and rib-vaulting. For the full effect, walk around the moat then climb onto the roof and look down into the courtyard to compare the contrasting styles. While you are there, look out over the city and the bay for one of the best views in Palma (Bellver means 'lovely view' in Catalan).

*Looking down on the circular courtyard of Bellver Castle*

For many centuries the castle was used as a prison; Jaume III's widow and sons were incarcerated here for most of their lives. These days it contains Palma's museum of municipal history which traces the development of the city through its artefacts, with pottery from Talaiotic, Roman, Arab and Spanish periods.

You can get there by car or taxi, or by bus to Plaça Gomila, climbing through the woods above Carrer de Bellver.

# Palma's Fundació la Caixa

## INFORMATION

➕ B2

✉ Plaça Weyler 3

☎ 971 720111

🕐 Tue–Sat 10–9, Sun 10–2

🍴 Café and restaurant (££)

♿ Good

✋ Free

**A quality hotel in the *modernista* style, dating from the turn of the 20th century, has been lovingly restored and is now an art gallery.**

The Gran Hotel was Palma's first luxury hotel when it opened in 1903. Designed by the Catalan architect Lluís Domènech i Montaner, it was the building that began the craze for *modernista* (art nouveau) architecture in the city. Restored by the Fundació la Caixa and reopened in 1993, the art gallery has changing exhibitions and a permanent display of paintings by Hermen Anglada-Camarasa, the founder of the 'Pollença school'. On the ground floor there is a bookshop and a trendy café-bar.

*Artistry can be admired inside and out at Fundació la Caixa – the 'in' place to meet for coffee and cakes*

## Palma's La Seu

**The glory of Palma – a magnificent Gothic cathedral whose sandstone walls and flying buttresses seem to rise out of the sea.**

Anything you see inside Palma cathedral will come as a disappointment once you have stood on the seafront and gazed up at its golden sandstone exterior, climbing above the old city walls. La Seu stands out utterly from its surroundings, a demonstration of the might of Mallorca's Christian conquerors to all who arrived by sea. Tradition has it that a storm arose as Jaume I was sailing towards Mallorca. He vowed that if he landed safely he would build a great church in honour of the Virgin. On New Year's Day 1230, a day after the fall of Palma, the foundation stone was symbolically laid on the site of the city's main mosque. Work continued for 400 years – and had to be resumed in 1851 when an earthquake destroyed the west front. More touches were added by the Catalan architect Antoni Gaudí.

You enter through a side door, passing a small museum; head for the west portal and gaze down the long nave. Light pours in through one of the world's largest rose windows, 12m across and studded with 1,236 pieces of stained glass. The columns are ringed with wrought-iron candelabra by Gaudí; his most controversial addition is the unfinished *Crown of Thorns*, fashioned from cardboard and cork and suspended above the altar. Be sure to walk around to the south front, facing the sea, to look at the Portal del Mirador, a 15th-century door by Guillem Sagrera featuring scenes from the Last Supper.

### INFORMATION

- ✚ B2
- ✉ Plaça d'Almoina
- ☎ 971 723130
- 🕐 Apr–Oct, Mon–Fri 10–6, Sat 10–2; Nov–Mar, Mon–Fri 10–3, Sat 10–2
- ♿ Few
- 💰 Cheap (free for services)
- ↔ Palau de l'Almudaina (➤ 38)
- ❓ High Mass, Sun 10:30

*A statue standing in a niche on the façade of the cathedral*

3

# Palma's Palau de l'Almudaina

## INFORMATION

🔢 B2

✉ Carrer Palau Reial

☎ 971 727145

🕐 Palace: Apr–Sep, Mon–Fri 10–6:30, Sat 10–2; Oct–Mar, Mon–Fri 10–2, 4–6, Sat 10–2
Gardens: open access

♿ Wheelchair access on request

💶 Palace: moderate
Gardens: free

❓ Still used by King Juan Carlos for official functions in Palma

**The imposing palace of Almudaina (meaning 'citadel') was once the residence of the kings of Mallorca, and is still used by today's Spanish royal family.**

A royal palace has stood here since the Muslim *walis* (governors) built their *alcázar* (fortress) after the Arab conquest. It was converted into Gothic style under Jaume II, but elements of Islamic architecture remain – like the Moorish arches seen from the seafront, lit up at night like a row of lanterns. The courtyard, laid out in 1309 and flanked by palm trees, is seen at its best in late afternoon when the sun falls on the cathedral towers. Off the courtyard is the royal chapel, Capella de Santa Ana.

The S'Hort del Rei gardens beneath the palace make a pleasant spot to sit and from here you can watch the world go by. Look for the Arc de la Drassana, once the gateway to the royal docks; near by is a statue of a *hondero* or Balearic slinger. The gardens were rebuilt in the 1960s and their best-known landmark is Joan Miró's *Egg* sculpture, which few people can resist sticking their heads through.

*The Islamic style of Palma's royal palace reflects its origins as a Muslim fortress*

# Pollença

**The attractions of Pollença have long been a magnet for tourists, but the town has learned to accept and adapt to tourism while still preserving its individuality.**

Located at the eastern end of the Serra de Tramuntana and tucked between two hills, each topped by a sacred site, Pollença is the perfect Mallorcan town. Large enough to avoid being twee but small enough to wander round in a morning, it has none of the feel of other towns which have succumbed under the sheer weight of tourism. Café life is still the rule; if you want to join in, come on a Sunday morning when the Plaça Major is filled with market stalls and, after church, the locals congregate to relax in the nearby Café Espanyol.

The Pont Romà (Roman bridge) on the edge of town is a clue to Pollença's long history. The name Pollença dates from the 14th century, when settlers from Alcúdia named the town after their former Roman capital. From the former Jesuit convent, now the town hall, you climb 365 steps, lined with cypress trees, to the Calvari church, with its ancient wooden cross and views of Puig de Maria. The church steps are the scene of a moving procession each Good Friday, when a figure of Christ is taken down from a cross and carried down the steps by torchlight.

The **Municipal Museum** in the former Dominican convent contains the remains of prehistoric sculptures shaped like bulls, as well as a *mandala* (Tibetan sand painting) given by the Dalai Lama in 1990. The cloisters of the convent are the venue for Pollença's celebrated classical music festival.

## INFORMATION

- 🔁 D1
- 🍴 Cafés and restaurants (££)
- 🚌 From Palma
- 🔁 Port de Pollença (➤ 40)
- ❓ Market held Sun; classical music festival, Jul–Sep; *Devallement* procession, Good Fri; *Moros i Cristians*, mock battle, 2 Aug

**Municipal Museum**
- ☎ 971 531166
- 🕐 Tue–Sun 11–1
- 💶 Cheap

*Climbing the Calvari steps on the way to salvation, with Puig de Maria in the background*

39

# Port de Pollença

**The ambience of Port de Pollença was captured by British crime writer Agatha Christie in *Problem at Pollensa Bay* (1936); its waterfront hotels were favoured by those in search of casual flirtations on the beach.**

This genteel, old-fashioned resort at the mouth of Pollença bay is particularly popular with families, and with older visitors in winter. There is also a large community of foreign residents, mostly retired British. The promenade along Passeig Voramar, all whitewashed villas and pine trees leaning into the sea, is perfect for an early evening walk. Look out for the bust of Hermen Anglada-Camarasa, the Catalan painter who spent many years in Pollença and whose work is displayed in the Fundació la Caixa in Palma (➤ 36). A favourite walk from Port de Pollença is the 3km hike across the Formentor peninsula through the Bóquer valley, a paradise for ornithologists and lovers of wild flowers.

*The brightly coloured sails of dinghies line the beach at Port de Pollença*

## Puig de Randa

**The steep ascent to Puig de Randa's three hermitages is repaid by the chance to experience the sense of awe and sanctity which still surrounds this table mountain that rises 543m out of the plain.**

### INFORMATION

- D3
- ☎ 971 120260
- 🍴 Restaurant at Santuari de Cura (££)
- 🖐 Free
- ❓ Simple rooms are available in a modern pilgrims' block

This mountain has been a place of pilgrimage ever since Ramón Llull (▶9) founded Mallorca's first hermitage here in 1275. He came aged 40, shaken by an incident which caused him to review his way of life. Bent on seduction he chased a married woman through Palma; unable to shake him off, she lifted her blouse to reveal cancerous breasts. Llull retired in isolation to Puig de Randa to ponder a life of youthful excess. These days pilgrims here are as likely to be weekend cyclists in search of a challenge as seekers after religious truth. The winding road to the summit leads to three separate hermitages. The lowest, Oratori de Nostra Senyora de Gràcia, is perched on a ledge in the cliff above a sheer 200m drop. Further up is the Santuari de Sant Honorat and finally Santuari de Cura, where Llull lived. The sense of history is offset by the radio mast on the mountain-top and the electric candles in the church, but this is still a special place. Visit the Sala Gramàtica to see Llull's original manuscripts and a bottle of 1934 Chartreuse made in the monastery, then look out from the terrace at the views of the plain, with Palma Bay and the isle of Cabrera in the distance.

*Ramón Llull, who retreated to a life of seclusion at the hermitage of Puig de Randa*

41

# S'Albufera

## INFORMATION

- D1–D2
- Carretera Port d'Alcúdia–Artà, km5
- 971 892250
- Apr–Sep, daily 9–7; Oct–Mar, daily 9–5
- Picnic area
- From Port d'Alcúdia to Cala Rajada in summer
- Free
- Alcúdia (► 24)
- Cars are not allowed in the reserve – leave them 1km from the visitor centre on the main road in the car park opposite Hotel Parc Natural

*Get away from it all with a day at S'Albufera, walking among the marshes and listening to the birds*

**The result of conservation initiatives in 1985 is this excellent wetland nature reserve, which is famous especially for its extraordinary variety of resident and migratory birdlife.**

Just off the coast road 5km south of Port d'Alcúdia, the S'Albufera wetlands make a welcome relief from long stretches of crowded beach. Birdwatchers come from all over Europe to see rare migrants like Montagu's harriers and Eleanora's falcons; species breeding here include stonechats, moustached warblers and the long-eared owl. Ospreys leave their breeding sites on the cliffs to come here to fish; peregrines and hoopoes live here all year round. The name S'Albufera derives from the Arabic for 'lagoon', but the site has been exploited since Roman times – Pliny writes of night herons, probably from S'Albufera, being sent to Rome as a gastronomic delicacy. The wetlands were drained for agriculture in the 19th century by a British company which subsequently went bankrupt; the network of canals dates from this

time. Rice was introduced in the early 20th century, paper was manufactured from the reeds and sedge, and it is only since 1985, following fears that tourist development was damaging the area's fragile ecology, that S'Albufera has been a protected nature reserve. There are footpaths, cycle trails, birdwatching hides and an audio-visual display room where you can listen to birdsong.

## Sa Calobra

**Once accessible only by sea, the small cove of Sa Calobra can now be reached via a remarkable winding road, making the journey almost as spectacular as the destination.**

Do not believe anyone who tells you that they have discovered the perfect unspoilt cove on the north coast – at least, not if its name is Sa Calobra. This is indeed a beautiful spot, but it cannot be described as secluded – buses filled with tourists pour in by the dozen every day, even in winter.

The journey to Sa Calobra is as memorable as the bay itself. A twisting road around Puig Major plunges 800m in just 12km, turning 270 degrees at one point to loop under itself (a feature known as the 'Knotted Tie'). The easier approach is by boat from Port de Sóller, passing genuinely isolated bays with an excellent view of Puig Major, albeit spoilt by the military installations on the summit of Mallorca's highest mountain.

Once there, walk through 200m of tunnels to reach the Torrent de Pareis ('twin streams'), which begins several kilometres up in the mountains at the confluence of the torrents of Lluc and Gorg Blau. Up to 400m high and only 30m wide, with some sections never seeing daylight, this dramatic gorge culminates in a small pebble beach where you can picnic among the crowds. In summer, when the gorge is dry, you can hike inland between the cliffs; do not attempt this in winter.

A side turn off the road to Sa Calobra leads to Cala Tuent, a small cove with a sandy beach and a 13th-century church, Ermita de Sant Llorenç. Cala Tuent is likely to be quieter than Sa Calobra; but don't believe anyone who tells you they have discovered the real unspoilt cove…

### INFORMATION

- C1
- Several restaurants (£–££)
- From Port de Sóller (all year, ☎ 971 633109)
- Lluc (► 33), Port de Sóller (► 55)
- Choral concert on the beach in Jul, ☎ 971 171958)

# Serra de Tramuntana

**The 'mountains of the north wind', which run the length of Mallorca's north coast, contain some of the island's most spectacular landscapes.**

The pine-covered slopes of the Serra de Tramuntana almost lean into the sea; as you climb higher, forested hills give way to barren crags and peaks. The people of Mallorca have good reason to be grateful to the mountains. In winter they act as a buffer, shielding the plain from the fierce *tramuntana* wind and absorbing most of the island's rain and snow; in summer they provide a cool retreat from the heat of Palma and the south.

*The Gorg Blau reservoir in the Serra de Tramuntana mountains*

The Serra de Tramuntana runs for 88km from Andratx to Pollença, with the rocky outcrops of Sa Dragonera and Cap de Formentor at either end. Of ten peaks over 1,000m, most are concentrated in the area around Lluc; the highest are Puig Major (1,445m) and Puig Massanella (1,349m). There are no rivers, though there are several mountain torrents which swell rapidly after rain – the Cúber and Gorg Blau reservoirs are essential resources on an island so often affected by drought.

The mountains are best explored slowly, on foot; you can smell the wild rosemary, hear the sheep-bells, see the goats, breathe in the air and marvel at pine trees growing out of red rock, nature's version of the colours of Mallorcan village houses. Take care when driving – these are the most dangerous roads on the island, with an endless procession of hairpin bends. The most dramatic drive of all is the C710 from Sóller to Lluc, traversing tunnels and gorges on its way from Puig Major to Puig Massanella.

# Sineu

**A lively weekly market takes over the town of Sineu – observe or join in the enthusiastic haggling, then visit the art gallery in the converted station.**

Sineu, at the geographical centre of Mallorca, comes alive each Wednesday morning at the island's most traditional market. It takes place on several levels. The sound of bleating leads you to the livestock market, where weather-beaten farmers haggle over the price of sheep before heading for the town's *celler* restaurants for an early brunch. Further up, on the way to the church, you pass the symbol of Sineu, a winged lion; near here are numerous stalls selling leather, lace and pearls. Eventually you reach Sa Plaça, the church square, where the action is liveliest of all, as housewives turn out to buy the week's food. Bags of snails, strings of tomatoes, buckets of olives – they are all here, along with plenty of fresh fruit, vegetables and flowers. It's best to get to Sineu early, before the tour buses arrive, to catch the flavour of a traditional country market. Among the best buys at the market are dried figs and apricots, pottery from Pòrtol and baskets – surprisingly, from Sudan. Also in Sineu is **S'Estació**, an unusual modern art gallery based in the old station.

## INFORMATION

🔢 D2
🍴 Several restaurants (££)
❓ Market held Wed

**S'Estació**
✉ Carrer Estació 2
☎ 971 520750
🕐 Mon–Fri 9:30–1:30, 4–7, Sat 9–1
🎟 Free

*The winged lion, honouring St Mark, is the symbol of Sineu*

# Sóller

## INFORMATION

- C2
- Wide choice of bars and restaurants (£–££)
- From Palma; tram to Port de Sóller
- Fornalutx (► 50), Port de Sóller (► 55)
- Market held Sat; *Moros i Cristians*, re-enactment of a 1561 battle in which local women helped to defeat a band of Turkish pirates, 8–10 May

**Natural Science Museum**
- Carretera Palma–Port de Sóller
- 971 634064
- Apr–Sep, Tue–Sat 10–8, Sun 10:30–1:30; Oct–Mar, Tue–Sat 10–5:30, Sun 10:30–1:30
- Cheap

**Museu Municipal**
- Carrer del Mar 9
- 971 634663
- Mon 11–5, Tue–Fri 10–6, Sat 10–2
- Cheap

**Set in a lush valley of orange groves between mountains and sea, Sóller is popular with day-trippers, who arrive on the vintage train from Palma.**

Visitors to Sóller from Palma (► 34) seem content to do little but sit outside the cafés in Plaça Constitució soaking up the atmosphere and the sun. With several *tapas* bars to choose from, and a fine selection of pastry-shops offering local ice cream and freshly squeezed orange juice, once you arrive here there is little temptation to move on.

The results of Sóller's wealth can be seen in its extravagant *modernista* architecture. The church of Sant Bartomeu has a 1912 arched tower suspended above the rose window, with spires like huge needles pointing into the air. The same architect, Gaudí's pupil Joan Rubió, designed the Banco Central Hispano next door.

A stroll to the cemetery above the station gives a clue to Sóller's history. Several of the epitaphs are in French, revealing the significant French community, descendants of those who came to make their fortune by exporting oranges.

Sóller has two museums worth visiting. The **Natural Science Museum**, in a turn-of-the-19th-century manor house on the Palma road, has a collection of fossils and a botanical garden. The **Museu Municipal** is an 18th-century house in the town centre, filled with antiques and relics of old Sóller.

A final word of advice: it is advisable to make your visit to Sóller by train, rather than by car. The climb over the Coll de Sóller is the most terrifying drive in Mallorca – it includes 57 hairpin bends. A controversial new road tunnel now runs through the mountain, but the train journey from Palma is a real delight, so why not leave the car behind and give yourself a treat?

## Son Marroig

**The former home of Archduke Ludwig Salvator has now become a lasting memorial to one whose devotion to Mallorca is legendary.**

Of all the famous foreigners attracted to Mallorca's northwest coast, none is so admired locally as 'S'Arxiduc', Archduke Ludwig Salvator. Born in 1847 in the Pitti Palace, Florence, the son of Leopold III of Tuscany and Marie Antoinette de Bourbon, he came to Mallorca 20 years later to escape from Viennese court life and immediately fell in love with the island. An ecologist before it was fashionable, and an early hippy who wore Mallorcan peasant clothes, he bought up estates along the coast in an effort to save them from development, and devoted himself to studying and recording Mallorcan wildlife and traditions. His seven-volume *Las Baleares* took 20 years to produce and is still an authority on its subject. He died in 1915 in a Bohemian castle.

The Archduke's home at Son Marroig, outside Deià, has been turned into a shrine to his memory, with his photographs, paintings and books and a museum devoted to his life. In the gardens is a white marble rotunda, made from Carrara marble and imported from Italy, where you can sit and gaze at the Na Foradada ('pierced rock') peninsula, jutting out to sea with a gaping 18m hole at its centre. Ask at the house for permission to walk onto the peninsula.

### INFORMATION

- 🔲 B2
- ✉ Carretera Valldemossa–Deià
- ☎ 971 639158
- 🕐 Mon–Sat 9:30–2, 3–6
- 🍴 Mirador de Na Foradada (££)
- 🚌 From Palma, Valldemossa and Port de Sóller
- 💷 Cheap
- ↔ Deià (➤ 30)
- ❓ Sunset concerts in summer

*From the rotunda in the Archduke's garden you can look down over the peninsula of Na Foradada*

# Valldemossa

## INFORMATION

- ✚ B2
- 🍴 Restaurants and bars (££)
- 🚌 From Palma, Deià and Port de Sóller
- ❓ Regular Chopin concerts in Palau del Rei Sanç (same ticket as monastery); La Beata procession in honour of Santa Catalina Thomás, 27–28 Jul; Chopin Festival in Aug; market held Sun

**Reial Cartoixa**
- ☎ 971 612106
- 🕐 Mar–Oct, Mon–Sat 9:30–6, Sun 10–1; Nov–Feb, Mon–Sat 9:30–4:30, Sun 10–1
- 💰 Expensive

*Locally-produced oranges are strung around a tree in Valldemossa's market*

**Valldemossa is the focus of the 'Chopin experience' in Mallorca, but it has more to offer, including an excellent modern art museum housed within a Carthusian monastery.**

Try as it might – and it doesn't try very hard – Valldemossa cannot escape its connection with Frédéric Chopin and his lover George Sand. They arrived in 1838, having rented a former monk's cell, planning to carry on their affair away from the gossip of Paris and hoping that the climate would benefit Chopin's health (he had tuberculosis). Nothing worked out as they had intended. The weather was wet and windy, the couple were shunned by the locals, Chopin's piano failed to arrive and the relationship never recovered. Sand vented her anger in a spiteful book, *Winter in Majorca*, which the locals, who were labelled as thieves and savages by the author, still gleefully sell to visitors.

In the **Reial Cartoixa** (Royal Carthusian Monastery) white-arched corridors lead to 'cells' containing museums on various themes. Visit the old pharmacy – you can almost smell the herbs – then look into the library, where the monks would meet for half an hour a week, their only human contact. There is a fine modern art museum, with works by Picasso, Miró and Juli Ramis, and of course there is Chopin's cell…

Valldemossa is also the birthplace of Catalina Thomás, Mallorca's patron saint. Born in 1531, she became a nun in Palma and was renowned for her humility. Almost every home in Valldemossa has a plaque imploring her prayers, and her birthplace at Carrer Rectoría 5 has been turned into a shrine. She would probably be appalled.

The newest attraction in Valldemossa is Michael Douglas' Costa Nord (➤ 78).

# MALLORCA's
## best

# Small Towns and Villages

---
**In the Top 25**

**⑥ CASTELL D'ALARÓ (➤ 28)**
**㉓ SÓLLER (➤ 46)**
---

## CALA FIGUERA

More than anywhere else in Mallorca, Cala Figuera retains the atmosphere of a working fishing port. A path follows around the tiny harbour and onto the cliffs, offering good views back towards the bay. The nearest beach is 4km to the south at Cala Santanyí.

➕ E3 🍴 Several seafood restaurants and others (££) 🚌 From Palma and Santanyi

## CAPDEPERA

This small town is crowned by the largest fortress in Mallorca. The Romans built the first castle on this site – the Moors enlarged it, the Christians destroyed it, then replaced it with one of their own in the 14th century. Legend has it that the besieged citizens of Capdepera hid in the castle, placing an image of Our Lady of Hope on the battlements, and the invaders were driven away by fog. The miracle is remembered each year at the town's annual *festa*. You reach the castle by climbing the steps from the market square.

➕ F2 🍴 Café de l'Orient, Plaça de l'Orient (£) 🚌 From Palma and Cala Rajada ❓ Market held Wed; Nostra Senyora de la Esperança festa, 18 Dec
**Castle** ☎ 971 818746 🕐 Apr–Oct, daily 10–8; Nov–Mar, daily 10–5 💷 Cheap

*Is Fornalutx the prettiest village in Spain? Go and judge for yourself*

## FORNALUTX

Fornalutx, in the hills above Sóller, calls itself the prettiest village in Spain, and it is hard to disagree. There are several terrace restaurants and bars, where you can sit and soak up the views of olive and orange groves climbing ever higher until they reach the pine-clad foothills of Puig Major.

➕ C2 🍴 Several restaurants (££)

## GALILEA

This pretty village, 460m above sea level, in the shadow of the great peak of Puig de Galatzó, is popular with day-trippers. From the church terrace you can see far out to sea, while eating *tapas* outside the church and listening to the echo of sheep-bells on the hillsides. The nearby village of Puigpunyent, surrounded by orange groves, is the base for visiting the nature reserve of La Reserva.

➕ B2 🍴 Two bars (£)

### INCA

Mallorca's third-largest town styles itself 'city of leather'. The best bargains can be found on Thursdays, at the weekly market around Plaça d'Espanya. Plenty of leather here, of varying quality, plus jewellery, carved olive-wood, lace and fresh produce from across the island. Plaça d'Espanya itself becomes an open-air flower show. Inca is also known for its *cellers*, old wine-cellars turned into restaurants featuring traditional dishes at reasonable prices.

🔀 C2 🍴 Wide choice of restaurants (££) 🚌 From Palma 🚉 From Palma 🔄 Binissalem ❓ Market held Thu

### MURO

Muro's overriding attraction is the Museu Etnòlogic de Mallorca, which gives fascinating glimpses into Mallorca's past. The kitchen contains pottery similar to what you see in the markets today; the recreated pharmacy has a pair of scales in the shape of a crucifix. Upstairs there is a fine collection of *siurells* (clay whistles) featuring men on horseback.

Sa Pobla, 4km north of Muro, is Mallorca's vegetable basket; this fertile area of reclaimed marshes is referred to as 'the land of a thousand windmills'. It is also the home of one of Mallorca's most unusual festivals, the Revelta de Sant Antoni.

🔀 D2 🍴 Bars and cafés (£) 🚉 From Palma ❓ Market held Sun; Revelta de Sant Antoni, 16–17 Jan

**Museu Etnòlogic de Mallorca**

✉ Carrer Major 15 ☎ 971 717540 🕐 Apr–Sep, Tue–Sat 10–2, 5–8, Sun 10–1; Oct–Mar, Tue–Sat 10–1, 4–6, Sun 10–1 💷 Cheap

### ORIENT

One of Mallorca's tiniest hamlets, with a population of less than 30, Orient nestles among olive trees at the foot of Puig d'Alfàbia. Numerous walks start from here, including an ascent to Castell d'Alaró; weekend day-trippers come from Palma to visit its three restaurants for Sunday lunch.

🔀 C2 🍴 Three good restaurants (££) 🔄 Castell d'Alaró (➤ 28)

### PETRA

This sleepy town of sand-coloured houses would be completely off the tourist map if it were not the birthplace of Mallorca's most famous son, Fray Junípero Serra. Born in 1713, he worked as a missionary first in Mexico and then in California, where the missions he established grew into cities such as San Diego and San Francisco. You can visit the house where Serra's parents lived, a museum devoted to his life and work, and the church of Sant Pere, where you can see the font in which he was baptised and there is a plaque to his memory.

🔀 D2 🍴 Es Celler restaurant (££); bars on main square (£) 🚌 From Palma 🔄 Ermita de Bonany (➤ 52) ❓ Market held Wed

**Serra House and Museum**

✉ Carrer Barracar Alt ☎ 971 561149 🕐 By arrangement – follow the directions to the keyholder's house 💷 Donation requested

*The house in Petra where Junípero Serra was born has been preserved to look much as it would have done in the 18th century*

51

# Hermitages and Sacred Sites

### DID YOU KNOW ?

*Bon any* means good year. The first church was built at Bonany in 1604; five years later, during a drought, the villagers of Petra climbed to the chapel to pray for rain. When their prayers were answered with a *Bon any*, they named their sanctuary Bonany.

### ERMITA DE BONANY

This hilltop hermitage is where Junípero Serra preached his last sermon in Mallorca before leaving to found the Mexican and Californian missions. The views from the terrace, covering almost the entire plain, are superb. You can stay here in simple cells, but unlike other monasteries it has no restaurant or bar – just a chapel and a shop selling religious trinkets.

➕ D2 ☎ 971 561101 🍴 Free 🔄 Petra (▶ 51)

### PUIG DE MARIA

Climb for an hour or two out of Pollença, or drive up a terrifying potholed road, and you are rewarded with views over Cap de Formentor and the entire northeastern coast. Nuns settled on Puig de Maria ('Mary's Mountain') in 1371 and remained for several hundred years, refusing to leave even when the Bishop of Palma ordered them down for their own safety. The convent is still there, on top of the mountain; the chapel smells of incense and the refectory of woodsmoke. You can stay in simple rooms in the sanctuary here, but don't expect luxury – you pay extra if you take a shower.

➕ D1 ☎ 971 184132 🍴 Bar-restaurant (£) 🚌 From Palma to Pollença 🍴 Free 🔄 Pollença (▶ 39)

*The views from the Santuari de Sant Salvador stretch right across the central plain*

### SANTUARI DE SANT SALVADOR

This old hermitage, 509m above sea level at the highest point of the Serra de Llevant, was the senior house of Mallorca's monastic order and the last to

lose its monks, in 1992. It is still a popular place of pilgrimage, flanked by two enormous landmarks – to one side a 14m stone cross, to the other a 35m column topped by a statue of Christ holding out his right hand in blessing. The church contains a fine carved alabaster retable, but more interesting is the side chapel off the gatehouse, full of poignant mementos and prayers to Our Lady. Like other former monasteries, San Salvador has a few simple rooms available for pilgrims.

➕ E3 ✉ Signposted from Felanitx–Porto Colom road ☎ 971 827282 🍴 Bar-restaurant (£) and picnic tables 🍴 Free

# Historic Sites

## CAPOCORB VELL

These are the most significant remains of the Talaiotic culture, which flourished in Mallorca between around 1300 and 800 BC. Villages were dominated by *talaiots*, circular or rectangular structures two to three storeys high, which were used as both burial chambers and defensive forts. At Capocorb Vell you can see five *talaiots* and wander around the ancient village.

➕ C3 ✉ Carretera Cap Blanc–Llucmajor ☎ 971 180155 🕐 Fri–Wed 10–5 🍴 Near by (£) 🎟 Cheap

## PALMA'S BANYS ÀRABS (ARAB BATHS)

These 10th-century baths are virtually all that remain of the Arab city of Medina Mayurqa; they were probably part of a nobleman's house. The *tepidarium* has a dome in the shape of a half-orange, with 25 round shafts for sunlight, supported by a dozen columns. *Hammams* were meeting places as well as wash-houses, and it would have been pleasant to cool off in the courtyard with its cactus, palm and orange trees.

➕ B2 ✉ Carrer Can Serra 7 ☎ 971 721549 🕐 Daily 9–8 🍴 Bar Sa Murada near by (£) ♿ None 🎟 Cheap

## PALMA'S BASÍLICA DE SANT FRANCESC

The façade of this 13th-century church is typically Mallorcan – a massive, forbidding sandstone wall with a delicately carved portal and a rose window at the centre. Inside is the tomb of Ramón Llull (► 41), whose statue can be seen on the seafront at Palma.

➕ B2 ✉ Plaça Sant Francesc ☎ 971 712695 🕐 Mon–Sat 9:30–12:30, 3:30–6, Sun 9:30–12:30 🎟 Cheap

## SES PAÏSSES

Although not as extensive as the ruins at Capocorb Vell (► above), this Bronze Age settlement near Artà is still a significant site, with its massive entrance portal, formed from three stone slabs weighing up to eight tonnes each. Inside there are several rooms and an *atalaia* (watchtower); the entire settlement is surrounded by a Cyclopean drystone wall.

➕ E2 🕐 Apr–Sep, daily 9–1, 3–7; Oct–Mar, Mon–Fri 9–1, 2:30–5, Sat 9–1 🚌 From Cala Rajada or Palma then a short walk 🚏 Artà (► 25) 🎟 Cheap

*An impressive baroque portal gives relief to the stern façade of Palma's mighty Basílica de Sant Francesc*

# Resorts

### CALA D'OR

Each of the various *calas* (bays) along the east coast has its own distinctive character; in the case of Cala d'Or the word is 'chic'. Former fishing harbours have been turned into marinas; people come here to sail and dive, and drink champagne at waterfront bars. The villas are white and flat-roofed, in Ibizan style, designed in the 1930s by Pep Costa Ferrer, and the effect is surprisingly attractive. Nowadays Cala d'Or is the collective name for a string of resorts, beaches and coves; they include Porto Petro, around a horseshoe bay 2km to the south, and Cala Mondragó, a further 4km south, where a pair of sandy beaches form part of the Mondragó nature reserve.

**+** E3 **▮▮** Wide choice of restaurants (££–£££) **🚌** From Palma

### PALMA NOVA

There are people who can remember when this was just a village; then along came the tourist boom, and 'new Palma' became the favoured resort of the British. More restrained than Magaluf, less exclusive than Portals Nous, Palma Nova occupies a prime position on the western side of the bay of Palma. It makes a good base for a family holiday, with nearby attractions including Marineland and Aquapark (➤ 56–57) – as long as you don't mind sharing your family holiday with a thousand others.

**+** B3 **▮▮** Wide choice of restaurants (£–££) **🚌** Regular buses from Palma **↔** Magaluf, Portals Nous (➤ 26)

*Port d'Andratx, a favourite haunt of the yachting set*

### PORT D'ANDRATX

Dress up to come here, or you will feel seriously out of place. Port d'Andratx is one of Mallorca's classiest resorts, popular with the yachting fraternity and with film stars whose Italian-style villas can be seen climbing up the hillsides. But don't let that put you off; come here all the same. The harbour is one of the prettiest in Mallorca and a table at one of the waterside bars is really the perfect place to watch the sunset.

**+** A3 **▮▮** Wide choice of restaurants (££–£££) **🚌** From Andratx

### PORT DE SÓLLER

This small resort, set around a fish-shaped natural harbour, has the only beach of any note along the entire north coast. It is the starting point for several boat trips along the coast; the trip to Sa Calobra (➤ 43) is one of the few to run throughout the year. Port de Sóller is also a good base for walks. A climb of less than an hour brings you to Cap Gros lighthouse for panoramic views of the bay and the mountains behind; a longer path, through rock gardens and olive groves, connects with an old mule track from Deià to Sóller.

➕ B2 🍴 Wide choice of restaurants (££) 🚌 From Palma, Valldemossa and Deià 🚆 From Palma; tram from Sóller

### PORTO CRISTO

This was one of the main resorts on the east coast until Cala Millor came along. So much the better: with bigger and better beaches elsewhere, Porto Cristo has carved out a role as a friendly, family resort, taking advantage of a superb position at the end of a long, sheltered inlet. Once the port for Manacor, Porto Cristo was the only place in Mallorca to be caught up in the Spanish Civil War, when it was briefly captured by Republican forces in 1936. There is not much to do but swim, sunbathe and dine at the terrace restaurants which are perfectly placed to catch the lunchtime sun – but day-trippers come in droves to visit the nearby caves (➤ 58). Other nearby family attractions include an aquarium and a safari park (➤ 56–57).

➕ E2–E3 🍴 Wide choice of restaurants (££) 🚌 From Palma and Manacor ❓ Coves del Drac (➤ 58) ❓ Market held Sun

### SANT ELM

The main reason for visiting Sant Elm, a laid-back resort with a fine sandy beach, is for the views of the island of Sa Dragonera, said to resemble a dragon. You can take a boat to the island from the jetty at the end of the main street, or sit outside the fish restaurants on the same jetty.

A challenging walk from Sant Elm leads to the abandoned Trappist monastery of Sa Trapa. Set out on Avinguda de la Trapa and climb through coastal *maquis* and pine. The round trip takes about three hours; a shorter route is signposted beside the cemetery on the Sant Elm to Andratx road. Near here is the village of S'Arracó, built by Spanish settlers returning from the American colonies.

➕ A2 🍴 Choice of restaurants (££) 🚌 From Andratx or Peguera 🚢 From Port d'Andratx and Peguera in summer 🚢 Sa Dragonera (➤ 55)

### CALA DE SANT VICENÇ

This old-fashioned holiday resort has recently been given a facelift and is in danger of becoming chic. It is still very popular with Mallorcans, especially on summer weekends. Four small coves, each with their own beach, huddle together beneath Cavall Bernat, a limestone ridge which casts its shadow into the sea. A walk of around 45 minutes leads across the hills to Port de Pollença (➤ 40).

➕ D1 🍴 Bars and restaurants (£–£££) 🚌 Bus from Pollença

*From Sant Elm you can climb to an abandoned monastery or take a boat to Sa Dragonera*

# Children's Activities

Mallorca is well geared up for family holidays. There are lots of good sandy beaches with safe, shallow water and first-aid stations, and many of the resorts feature activities like crazy-golf courses and pony rides. Here is a selection of activities that will appeal to children.

## THEME PARKS AND WATERPARKS

### AQUACITY

One of the world's largest water funfairs. In addition to the water slides and wave pool there is a mini-zoo, as well as a children's farm, parrot shows and an antique typewriter museum.

✚ C3 ✉ S'Arenal (Platja de Palma); at end of Palma–S'Arenal motorway ☎ 971 440000 ◷ May–Sep, daily 10–5; Oct, Sun–Fri 10–5 🚌 23 from Palma via Platja de Palma

### AQUAPARK

There are pools, slides, a 'water castle' and exciting rides at this long-established waterpark situated on the edge of town.

✚ B3 ✉ Carretera Cala Figuera, Magaluf ☎ 971 130811 ◷ Jun–Sep, daily 10–6; May, Oct, daily 10–5

### HIDROPARK

A water-based theme park with activities for very young children as well as waterslides and wave pools

✚ D1 ✉ Avinguda Tucán, Port d'Alcúdia ☎ 971 891672 ◷ May–Oct, daily 10–6

### WESTERN PARK

'Crazy Wet West' is the slogan of this Wild West theme park in Magaluf, with cowboy and high-diving shows, thrilling water rides, playgrounds, fast food restaurants and video arcades.

✚ B3 ✉ Carretera Cala Figuera ☎ 971 131627 ◷ May–Oct, daily 10–6

## ANIMALS AND ZOOS

### ACUÀRIUM DE MALLORCA

A small aquarium with exotic fish from around the world including piranhas and electric eels. Located next to the Coves del Drac (➤ 58).

✚ E3 ✉ Carrer Vélla, Porto Cristo ☎ 971 820971 ◷ Apr–Oct, daily 10:30–5; Nov–Mar, daily 11–3

### EXOTIC PARQUE

Children love the performing parrots at this tropical garden. There are also flamingos and a children's zoo.

*Splash-down at Aquacity, one of Mallorca's best children's attractions*

🚩 E3 ✉ Carretera Porto Cristo– Porto Colom, Cales de Mallorca
☎ 971 183492 🕐 Apr–Oct, daily 10–7; Nov–Mar, daily 10–5

## MARINELAND

Entertainment here is provided by the performing
dolphins, sea lions and parrots. There is also a
penguin pool, a reptile house and a large collection of
sharks and tropical fish, plus flamingos, monkeys and
an impressive aviary. Children can ride on a mock
pirate boat and a miniature train. The little ones will
love it, but their parents may not – especially if they
are fond of dolphins. But whatever you think about
animal shows, Marineland is a success – and the
crowds it attracts generate handsome profits, which
are then put back into conservation programmes.
🚩 B3 ✉ Carretera Palma–Andratx km10, Portals Nous ☎ 971
675125 🕐 Apr–Sep, daily 9:30–6; Oct–Mar, daily 9:30–5. Closed
mid-Nov to Christmas 🚌 From Palma, Palma Nova, Magaluf, Santa
Ponça

## NATURA PARC

An easy walking trail leads around a wildlife park
where Mallorcan farm animals can be seen, along
with butterflies, black vultures and imported species
like pelicans and Chinese geese. There is also a
picnic area and café.
✉ Carretera de Sineu, km15 ☎ 971 144078 🕐 Daily 10–7

## NEMO SUBMARINES

See the flora and fauna beneath the sea on a 2-hour
exploration by mini-submarine. Very expensive.
🚩 B3 ✉ Carrer Galeón 2, Magaluf ☎ 971 130244 🕐 Mar–Oct
daily

## SAFARI-ZOO

Drive-round safari park with giraffes, zebra and
monkeys plus a 'baby zoo' with young elephants and
reptiles born here. Arrive early to see the feeding.
🚩 F2 ✉ Carretera Porto Cristo–Son Servera, km5, Cala Millor
☎ 971 810909 🕐 Apr–Sep, daily 9–7; Oct–Mar, daily 9–5
🚌 Free bus service from Cala Millor in summer

# MINI-GOLF

### GOLF FANTASIA (PALMA NOVA)

One of the best mini-golf courses, set amid waterfalls,
caves and tropical gardens. There is a choice of three
different circuits – or you can play all 54 holes. Even
adults will enjoy it.
🚩 B3 ✉ Carrer Tenis 3, Palma Nova ☎ 971 135040 🕐 Daily,
10–midnight in summer

### GOLF FANTASIA (PLATJA DE PALMA)

This is the sister course to the Palma Nova outlet, on
the other side of the island.
🚩 C3 ✉ Carretera Arenal 56, S'Arenal ☎ 971 743334
🕐 Daily, 9AM–midnight in summer

---

## LOOKING AFTER CHILDREN

Small children are particularly
vulnerable to the sun and
need to be well protected:
apply a high-factor sun block
regularly, especially after
swimming. If you need a child
seat in your rented car, be
sure to book it in advance and
then check it carefully on
arrival. The same goes for cots
and high-chairs in hotels and
apartments. Finally, don't
forget to check that your
balcony railings are secure.

*A trio of performing
dolphins at Marineland*

# Scenic Places

## BANYALBUFAR

People come to Banyalbufar to see one thing – its terraced hillsides, sloping down to the sea. Developed by the Moors and divided by drystone walls, these terraces speak powerfully of man's ingenuity in creating farmland out of inhospitable cliffs. Until recently it was the custom for each generation to add a further tier.

The terraced slopes of Banyalbufar, created over a thousand years, reach right down to the sea

➕ B2 🍴 Café Bellavista (£) 🚌 Bus from Palma 🔄 La Granja (➤ 32)

## COVES DEL DRAC (DRAGON CAVES)

Dank, dark and humid, these limestone caves on the edge of Porto Cristo have become one of Mallorca's top tourist sights. Several hundred people at a time are herded along 2km of slippery paths by guides; the tour ends with a floodlit, floating violin concert on Lake Martel, Europe's largest underground lake.

➕ E3 ☎ 971 820753 🕐 Apr–Oct, tours on the hour 10–5; Nov–Mar, tours at 10:45, 12, 2, 3:30 🍴 Café (£) 🚌 From Palma and Cala Rajada 🚫 None 💵 Expensive 🔄 Acuàrium de Mallorca (➤ 56)

## JARDINS DE ALFÁBIA

These classical gardens by the entrance to the Sóller tunnel are a legacy of the Arab talent for landscaping and irrigation. The name derives from *al fabi*, 'jar of olives' in Arabic. They were probably designed by Benihabet, the Muslim governor of Inca who converted to Christianity following the Spanish invasion.

➕ B2 ✉ Carretera Palma–Sóller, km14 ☎ 971 613123 🕐 Apr–Sep, Mon–Fri 9:30–6:30, Sat 9:30–1; Oct–Mar, Mon–Fri 9:30–5, Sat 9:30–1 🍴 Ses Porxeres (££) in the car park 💵 Moderate

## PALMA'S PARC DE LA MAR

Until the 1960s the sea reached up to the city walls, providing the perfect reflection for the cathedral. When the building of a new road changed all that, an artificial lake was constructed to reproduce the effect. The park around the lake is now a popular venue at weekends, with a Miró mural and an art gallery in the vaults of the old city walls.

➕ B2 ✉ On south side of the cathedral 🍴 Choice of cafés (£) 💵 Free ❓ Free concerts on summer evenings

# Free Attractions

*The furnaces and machinery in the Ca'n Gordiola glass factory are on view to visitors*

## CA'N GORDIOLA
Glass factory and museum, housed in a mock castle outside the town of Algaida. Watch the glass being made, then buy it in the shop next door.
✚ C2 ✉ Carretera Palma-Manacor, km19 ☎ 971 665046
🕐 Apr–Oct, Mon–Sat 9–8, Sun 9–1; Nov–Mar, Mon–Sat 9–1:30, 3–7, Sun 9–1

## CA'N SOLLERIC
This 18th-century seigneurial palace was built for a family of olive oil merchants. It now houses a contemporary art gallery whose ground-floor café is one of the trendiest meeting places in Palma.
✚ B2 ✉ Passeig des Born 27, Palma ☎ 971 722092
🕐 Tue–Sat 10–1:45, 5–8:30, Sun 10–1:45

## MUSEU JUNÍPERO SERRA
This small museum devoted to the 'founder of California' (▶ 9) is located in a house close to his birthplace in the village of Petra (▶ 51).
✚ D2 ✉ Carrer Barracar Alt, Petra ☎ 971 561149 🕐 By arrangement – follow directions to the keyholder's house (donation requested)

## PERLAS MAJÓRICA
Cultured pearls are one of Mallorca's best-known exports. Watch them being made at this pearl factory.
✚ E2 ✉ Avinguda Majórica 48, Manacor ☎ 971 550200
🕐 Mon–Fri 9–1, 2:30–7, Sat–Sun 10–1

## SES VOLTES
The art gallery in the military vaults of Palma's medieval walls has a comprehensive collection of 19th- and 20th-century Mallorcan paintings.
✚ B2 ✉ Parc de la Mar, Palma ☎ 971 714238 🕐 Mon–Sat 10–1:45, 5–8:45, Sun 10–1:45

## DOING THE *PASSEIG*

The best free entertainment in Mallorca consists of joining the locals on their early evening promenade (*paseo* in Spanish, *passeig* in Mallorquín). The most romantic *passeig* of all is along the Pine Walk in Port de Pollença, where the pine trees lean into the sea, the fishing boats bob in the bay and the various terrace bars tempt you in for an apéritif beside the beach.

# Places to Have Lunch

**BON LLOC (£)**

You won't find better value than this four-course vegetarian lunch.

➕ B2 ✉ Carrer Sant Feliu 7, Palma ☎ 971 718617 🕒 Closed Sun

**CABALLITO DE MAR (££–£££)**

Fish restaurant placed to catch the winter sun.

➕ B2 ✉ Passeig Sagrera 5, Palma ☎ 971 721074 🕒 Closed Mon

**CA N'ANTUNA (££)**

Dine on a terrace overlooking the orange groves.

➕ C2 ✉ Carrer Arbona Colom 8, Fornalutx ☎ 971 633068 🕒 Closed Mon

**CELLER SA FONT (££)**

Farmers go here after Sineu's Wednesday market.

➕ D2 ✉ Plaça d'Espanya 18, Sineu ☎ 971 520313 🕒 Daily

**CENTRO (£)**

Huge portions, excellent food, ridiculous prices.

➕ D3 ✉ Avinguda Bisbe Campins 13, Porreres ☎ 971 168372 🕒 Closed Sun

**LA GRAN TORTUGA (££)**

Eat and swim on a terrace overlooking the sea.

➕ A3 ✉ Aldea Cala Fornells 1, Peguera ☎ 971 686023 🕒 Closed Mon

**PUIG DE SANT MIQUEL (££)**

Roast kid and other Mallorcan specialities served beside a hilltop sanctury.

✉ Carretera de Manacor, km31 ☎ 971 646314 🕒 Daily

**STAY (£££)**

Fresh fish beside the harbour.

➕ D1 ✉ Moll Nou, Port de Pollença ☎ 971 864013 🕒 Daily

*Holidaymakers and locals enjoy a coffee in Palma's Plaça Major*

# MALLORCA
## where to...

# In Palma

## PRICES

Prices are approximate, based on a three-course meal for one, without drinks and service:

£   = under €12
££  = €12–24
£££ = over €24

Most restaurants serve a *menú del día* at lunchtime (➤ 66), which will usually work out much cheaper. It is normal practice to add about 10 per cent to the bill as a tip.

## A WARNING

Opening hours change frequently, and many restaurants take an annual holiday in winter. It is always a good idea to telephone before setting out.

### ARAMIS (£££)

Modern Mediterranean cuisine and weekly wine-tasting menu in a town house behind La Llotja.

✉ Carrer Montenegro 1
☎ 971 725232  🕐 Lunch, Mon–Fri, dinner Mon–Sat

### ASADOR TIERRA ASANDA (££)

Barbecued meat including suckling pig, lamb and kid in the setting of an old Palma mansion near Avinguda Jaume III.

✉ Carrer Concepció 4
☎ 971 714256  🕐 Lunch Tue–Sat, dinner Mon–Sat

### BAISAKHI (££)

Specialises in high-class Indian cuisine; try the gourmet menu with wine and *lassi* included.

✉ Passeig Marítim 8
☎ 971 736806
🕐 Lunch, dinner. Closed Mon

### LA BODEGUILLA (££)

Classic Castilian stews amid hanging wine bottles; the same owners have a stylish *tapas* bar next door.

✉ Carrer Sant Jaume 1 & 3
☎ 971 718274
🕐 Lunch, dinner. Closed Sun

### BON LLOC (£)

Vegetarian restaurant with four-course set lunch.

✉ Carrer Sant Feliu 7
☎ 971 718617  🕐 Lunch Mon–Sat, dinner Wed–Sat

### CABALLITO DE MAR (££)

Popular fish restaurant on the seafront – sit outside to catch the sun.

✉ Passeig Sagrera 5
☎ 971 721074
🕐 Lunch, dinner. Closed Mon

### CA'N CARLOS (££)

One of the few restaurants in central Palma to focus on traditional Mallorcan cuisine.

✉ Carrer de l'Aigua 5
☎ 971 713869
🕐 Lunch, dinner. Closed Sun

### CANDELA (£££)

In a street known for its *tapas* bars, this place offers fresh fish and creative Mediterranean cuisine.

✉ Carrer dels Apuntadors 14
☎ 971 724428  🕐 Lunch, dinner. Closed Wed

### CA'N EDUARDO (££)

Traditional fish restaurant above the fish market.

✉ Es Moll de Pescadors
☎ 971 721182  🕐 Lunch, dinner. Closed Sun

### CA'N JOAN DE S'AIGO (£)

Classy café where Joan Miró used to go for hot chocolate and *ensaimadas*.

✉ Carrer Sant Sanç 10  ☎ 971 710759  🕐 Closed Tue

### CELLER SA PREMSA (££)

Mallorcan classics in a converted garage lined with wine vats and faded bullfighting posters.

✉ Plaça Bisbe Berenguer de Palou 8  ☎ 971 723529
🕐 Lunch, dinner. Closed Sun

### CHOPIN (£££)

Top-notch Swiss-Mediterranean dishes on a garden terrace.

✉ Carrer Ca'n Puigdorfila 2
☎ 971 723556
🕐 Lunch, dinner. Closed Sun

### ES BALUARD (£££)

Modern versions of traditional Mallorcan

cooking – how about shoulder of lamb stuffed with *sobrasada* and aubergines?

✉ Plaça Porta Santa Catalina 9
☎ 971 719609
🕒 Lunch, dinner. Closed Sun

### FABRICA 23 (££)

One of the hottest restaurants in town is run by an English chef in the buzzing Santa Catalina district. Go early if you want a table at lunchtime.

✉ Carrer Fabrica 23
☎ 971 728077 🕒 Lunch, dinner, Tue–Sat

### FUNDACIÓ LA CAIXA (££)

Cocktails, cakes and serious meals in the bar of the former Gran Hotel.

✉ Plaça Weyler 3
☎ 971 728077 🕒 Lunch, dinner. Closed Sun dinner

### GADUS (££)

Salt cod with everything is the motto at this offbeat fish restaurant in Santa Catalina.

✉ Carrer Fábrica 5
☎ 971 450162 🕒 Lunch, dinner. Closed Sun

### GIOVANNI'S (££)

This busy Italian restaurant near La Llotja has become a Palma institution, popular with tourists and expats.

✉ Carrer Sant Joan 3
☎ 971 722879
🕒 Lunch, dinner. Closed Mon

### KOLDO ROYO (£££)

Specialising in Basque and Mallorcan *nouvelle cuisine*, with views of the bay.

✉ Passeig Marítim 3
☎ 971 732435 🕒 Lunch Mon–Sat, dinner Mon–Fri

### LA LUBINA (££)

Fish restaurant on the quay – try *lubina en sal*, sea bass baked in rock salt.

✉ Es Moll Vell ☎ 971 723350 🕒 Lunch, dinner

### NA BAUÇANA (£)

Friendly vegetarian restaurant with set-price midweek lunch.

✉ Carrer Santa Bàrbara 4
☎ 971 721886
🕒 Lunch Mon–Sat

### EL PILON (££)

Good *tapas* bar in an alley off the Born.

✉ Carrer Ca'n Cifre 3
☎ 971 717590
🕒 Lunch, dinner. Closed Sun

### S'ARROSSERIA (££)

Rice served in a dozen different styles, from 'convent rice' (vegetarian) to lobster paella.

✉ Passeig Marítim 13
☎ 971 737447
🕒 Lunch, dinner. Closed Mon

### S'OLIVERA (££)

Mediterranean cooking and a large range of *tapas* in the old Arab quarter.

✉ Carrer Morey 5 ☎ 971 712935 🕒 Lunch Mon–Sat, dinner Mon–Fri

### SA VOLTA (£)

Authentic cellar bar with hams hanging from the ceiling – one of numerous *tapas* bars along this street.

✉ Carrer dels Apuntadors 5
🕒 Lunch, dinner

### TABERNA DE LA BOVEDA (££)

Great *tapas* on a terrace facing the harbour.

✉ Passeig Sagrera 3 ☎ 971 720026 🕒 Lunch, dinner. Closed Sun

### TAPAS

*Tapas* are a Spanish institution. Originally a free 'lid' (*tapa*) of ham across a drink, nowadays they consist of small portions of everything from octopus to olives. Locals eat *tapas* before going out to eat, but several portions can make an unusual meal in itself. The best place to eat *tapas* in Mallorca is in the area around La Llotja in Palma.

# Around the Island

## EATING OUT IN MALLORCA

The Spanish like to eat late – many restaurants do not even open until 1:30 at lunchtime and 8:30 in the evening, and fill up an hour or two later. It is a good idea to book a table in advance, especially in summer and at weekends. Formal dress is rarely necessary – even at the best establishments smart casual is the rule. And children are always welcome!

## ALGAIDA

### CAL DIMONI (££)
Meat and blood sausages grilled over an open fire.
✉ Carretera Palma–Manacor, km21 ☎ 971 665035
🕐 Lunch, dinner. Closed Wed

### CA'N MATEU (££)
Roast suckling pig and other specialities; pool and children's play area.
✉ Carretera Palma–Manacor, km21 ☎ 971 665036
🕐 Lunch, dinner. Closed Tue

### ES 4 VENTS (££)
Mallorcan and Spanish classics, very popular for Sunday lunch.
✉ Carretera Palma–Manacor, km21 ☎ 971 665173
🕐 Lunch, dinner. Closed Thu

### HOSTAL D'ALGAIDA (££)
Mallorcan cuisine in an old coaching inn – try croquettes of spinach with monkfish.
✉ Carretera Palma–Manacor, km21 ☎ 971 665109
🕐 Lunch, dinner daily

## ARTÀ

### CAFÉ PARISIEN (££)
Coffee, pastries, salads and Mediterrranean cuisine in an arty café on the city's main street.
✉ Carrer Ciutat 18
☎ 971 835440
🕐 Lunch, dinner. Closed Sun

## BINISSALEM

### EL SUIZO (££)
Swiss fondues plus French and Mallorcan cuisine.
✉ Carrer Pou Bo 20
☎ 971 870076
🕐 Lunch, dinner. Closed Tue

## CALA MILLOR

### EL PESCADOR (££)
Harbourside restaurant specialising in paella as well as grilled meat and fish dishes.
✉ Port Cala Bona ☎ 971 586602 🕐 Lunch, dinner. Closed Wed

## CALA D'OR

### BLANCO Y NEGRO (££)
Stuffed squid and other seafood specialities served in a pleasant setting overlooking the marina.
✉ Marina de Cala d'Or ☎ 971 643465 🕐 Lunch, dinner

### PORT PETIT (£££)
Seafood and unusual desserts in a smart restaurant with views of the marina.
✉ Carrer Port Petit
☎ 971 643039 🕐 Dinner daily Apr–Oct

## CALA RAJADA

### SES ROTGES (£££)
Quality French cooking with prices to match, served in the restaurant at one of Mallorca's top hotels.
✉ Carrer Rafael Blanes 21
☎ 971 563108 🕐 Lunch, dinner. Closed Nov–Mar

## CALA DE SANT VIÇENC

### CAVALL BERNAT (£££)
Top-notch Mallorcan meat and fish dishes, such as spiced turbot and roast suckling lamb, plus a gourmet tasting menu.
✉ Carrer Maressers 2
☎ 971 530250 🕐 Dinner daily

## CALVIÀ

### CA NA CUCO (££)
Fresh, good-value Mallorcan cuisine in a restaurant popular with the locals.
✉ Avinguda de Palma 14 ☎ 971 670083 🕒 Lunch, dinner. Closed Mon. Dinner only Tue, Wed

### MESON CA'N TORRAT (££)
Mallorcan classics like *llom amb col* and roast shoulder of lamb in a rustic bar opposite the church.
✉ Carrer Església 5 ☎ 971 670682 🕒 Dinner. Closed Tue

## CAPDEPERA

### CAFÉ DE L'ORIENT (£)
Lively *tapas* bar on the market square – each dish is available in three different-sized portions.
✉ Plaça de l'Orient 4 ☎ 971 563098 🕒 Daily 8AM–midnight

## CASTELL D'ALARÓ

### ES VERGER (££)
Roast lamb cooked in a wood-fired oven at this farmhouse restaurant halfway up to the castle.
✉ On the way to Castell d'Alaró ☎ 971 182126 🕒 Lunch, dinner daily

## DEIÀ

### EL OLIVO (£££)
Fine *nouvelle cuisine* in a romantic setting – one of the best restaurants on the island for a special occasion.
✉ La Residencia hotel ☎ 971 639392 🕒 Lunch, dinner daily

### JAUME (££)
A Deià institution offering unchanging Mallorcan dishes like *tumbet* and *frit mallorquí* in defiance of the trends towards new Mallorcan cuisine.
✉ Carrer Arxiduc Lluis Salvador 13 ☎ 971 639029 🕒 Lunch, dinner. Closed Mon

### MIRADOR DE NA FORADADA (££)
Dine with a view of the northwest coast. Typical Mallorcan/Spanish cuisine.
✉ Son Marroig, Carretera Valldemossa–Deià ☎ 971 639026 🕒 Lunch, dinner. Closed Thu

### SEBASTIAN (£££)
Modern Mediterranean cooking with an emphasis on fresh fish in an old town house with bare stone walls.
✉ Carrer Felipe Bauza ☎ 971 639417 🕒 Dinner only. Closed Wed and Nov–Mar

## FORNALUTX

### CA'N ANTUNA (££)
Mallorcan cuisine on a shady terrace with views of orange groves and distant peaks.
✉ Carrer Arbona Colom 8 ☎ 971 633068 🕒 Lunch, dinner. Closed Mon

## INCA

### CELLER CA'N AMER (££)
This busy *celler* represented the best Balearic cooking at the Expo 92 fair in Seville.
✉ Carrer Pau 39 ☎ 971 501261 🕒 Lunch, dinner. Closed Sun

### CELLERS
A *celler* is an old wine cellar converted into a restaurant specialising in traditional Mallorcan cuisine. Real basement *cellers* have wine vats to prove it, but nowadays the term is used for any old-style restaurant.
*Cellers* are good places to go in order to try Mallorcan classics like *llom amb col* (pork wrapped in cabbage) or *frit mallorquí* (fried offal). The best *cellers* are found in market towns like Inca and Sineu.

# Around the Island

## MENÚ DEL DÍA

Most restaurants offer a *menú del día* at lunchtime – a set-price three-course meal with water or wine included. You won't get much choice (typically soup or salad, meat or fish and fruit or ice cream) but the food will be freshly cooked, filling and sometimes surprisingly good. A three-course lunch in a small rural town will often cost less than a single portion of *tapas* in Palma.

### JARDINES D'ALFÀBIA

**SES PORXERES (££)**
Catalan game dishes in a rustic barn beside the Alfàbia gardens.
✉ Carretera Palma–Sóller
☎ 971 613762
🕐 Lunch, dinner. Closed Sun dinner, Mon

### ORIENT

**L'HERMITAGE (£££)**
Choose between a flower-filled terrace or a dining-room full of antiques at this 17th-century manor house and hotel. The menu, based on fresh local ingredients, changes daily.
✉ Carretera Alaró–Bunyola
☎ 971 180303
🕐 Lunch, dinner

**HOSTAL DE MUNTANYA (££)**
*Pa amb oli* at lunchtime and modern Mallorcan cooking in the evening at this newly renovated hotel.
✉ Carretera de Bunyola
☎ 971 615373
🕐 Lunch, dinner

**MANDALA (££)**
Innovative French–Indian cuisine by a couple from Geneva, in a house at the very top of the village.
✉ Carrer Nou 1
☎ 971 615285 🕐 Jun–Aug, dinner Mon–Sat; Sep–May, lunch Tue–Sun, dinner Fri–Sat

**RESTAURANT ORIENT (££)**
Suckling pig is a speciality in this popular village bar.
✉ Carretera de Bunyola
☎ 971 615153 🕐 Lunch, dinner. Closed Sun dinner, Tue

### PALMA NOVA

**CIRO'S (££)**
Pizzas and other Italian/Mediterranean specialities are served on a terrace overlooking the beach.
✉ Passeig del Mar 3 ☎ 971 681052 🕐 Lunch, dinner

### PEGUERA

**LA GRAN TORTUGA (££)**
Seafood and European cuisine is served on a terrace overlooking a pretty bay – you can order your meal then take a dip in the swimming pool while it is being cooked.
✉ Aldea Cala Fornells 1
☎ 971 686023
🕐 Lunch, dinner. Closed Mon

**LA GRITTA (££)**
Chic Italian restaurant with an emphasis on seafood.
✉ Aldea Cala Fornells 2 ☎ 971 686022 🕐 Lunch, dinner

### PETRA

**ES CELLER (££)**
Typical Mallorcan *celler* bar with an olive press and hearty peasant cooking.
✉ Carrer de l'Hospital 46
☎ 971 561056 🕐 Lunch, dinner. Closed Mon

**SA PLAÇA (££)**
Prawns in chocolate sauce is just one of the old-style Mallorcan dishes being reinvented at this samll hotel-restaurant on the main square.
✉ Plaça Ramon Llull 4
☎ 971 561646 🕐 Lunch, dinner. Closed Tue

## PLATJA DE PALMA

### CA'N TORRAT (££)
A treat for serious carnivores – hunks of meat are barbecued over a fire in the garden.

✉ S'Arenal exit from motorway ☎ 971 262055 🕔 Lunch, dinner. Closed Wed

### RANCHO PICADERO (££)
Restaurant which specialises in meats cooked on wood fires.

✉ Carrer de Flamenc 1 ☎ 971 261002 🕔 Lunch, dinner. Closed Mon

## POLLENÇA

### CA'N PACIENCI (£££)
Sample the adventurous French-style cooking including duck in five different sauces.

✉ Carretera Port de Pollença ☎ 971 530787 🕔 Dinner only, Mon–Sat, Mar–Oct

### CANTONET (££)
Italian restaurant featuring salads, fresh pasta and vegetarian dishes.

✉ Carrer Montesió 20 ☎ 971 530429 🕔 Lunch, dinner in winter, dinner only in summer. Closed Tue

### CLIVIA (££)
This popular restaurant is in an old manor house – the speciality is roasted sea bass.

✉ Avinguda Pollentia 9 ☎ 971 533635 🕔 Lunch, dinner. Closed Tue, Wed lunch

### LA FONT DEL GALL (££)
French-style cooking in an intimate back-street restaurant close to the 'cockerel fountain' from which it takes its name.

✉ Carrer Montesió 4 ☎ 971 530396 🕔 Dinner, Apr–Oct

### IL GIARDINO (££)
Italian specialities – veal with mushrooms, salmon with lemon sauce.

✉ Plaça Major 11 ☎ 971 534302 🕔 Lunch, dinner

## PORT D'ALCÚDIA

### BOGAVANTE (£££)
The rice and fresh fish dishes are especially good at this seafood restaurant facing the harbour.

✉ Carrer Teodor Canet 2 ☎ 971 547364 🕔 Lunch Tue–Sun, dinner daily

### KHUM PHANIT'S (£)
This is a real surprise – authentic Thai cooking and extremely good value.

✉ Avinguda de la Platja 7 ☎ 971 548141 🕔 Lunch, dinner. Closed Mon lunch

## PORT D'ANDRATX

### MIRAMAR (£££)
Lobster and seafood beside the harbour – but you'll need to take out a mortgage before you come here.

✉ Avinguda Mateo Bosch 22 ☎ 971 671617 🕔 Lunch, dinner daily

### ROCAMAR (££)
This is the place to try Galician and Mallorcan seafood specialities in a perfect setting at the end of the promenade.

✉ Carrer d'Almirante Riera Alemany 29 ☎ 971 671261 🕔 Lunch, dinner daily

### FISH AND SEAFOOD

Mallorca's fish stocks have long been in decline and most of the fish on sale in Mallorca is imported from mainland Spain and beyond. By law, restaurant menus should state whether fish is fresh or frozen – prices for frozen fish are invariably cheaper. Fresh fish is always excellent; specialities include lobster casserole, sea bass in rock salt, and _greixonera de peix_, a hearty fish stew cooked in an earthenware bowl.

67

# Around the Island

## OLIVES

Olives were introduced to Mallorca by the Romans and have been used ever since – the oil for cooking and soap, the branches for firewood, the wood for carving into bowls and spoons. Almost every meal begins with bread and olives, for which you may pay a small charge. Bread and olives are also at the heart of *pa amb oli*, the favourite Mallorcan snack – bread rubbed with tomato, drizzled with olive oil and topped with ham or cheese.

## PORT DE POLLENÇA

### LA LLONJA DEL PESCADO (££)

Try the lobster stew at this harbour restaurant.
✉ Dique Moll ☎ 971 866504 🕐 Lunch, dinner

### STAY (£££)

This is a popular fish restaurant on the jetty – try the *parrillada*, a fish and seafood mixed grill.
✉ Moll Nou ☎ 971 864013 🕐 Lunch, dinner

## PORT DE SÓLLER

### CELLER D'ES PORT (££)

Enormous helpings of Mallorcan classics like roast shoulder of lamb with oregano.
✉ Carrer Antoni Montis 17 ☎ 971 630654 🕐 Lunch daily, dinner at weekends. Closed Wed

### FARO (££)

Fresh fish in a magnificent setting, high above the fishing port.
✉ Cap Gros de Maleta ☎ 971 633752 🕐 Lunch, dinner. Closed Tue

## PORTALS NOUS

### EL BISTRO DE TRISTAN (££)

More modest version of Tristan (this page), run by the same chef.
✉ Puerto Porttals marina ☎ 971 676141 🕐 Lunch, dinner. Closed Mon and Nov–Feb

### MESON SON CALIU (£)

Typically Mallorcan cuisine with a good-value *menú del día*.
✉ Carretera Palma–Andratx, km12 ☎ 971 680086 🕐 Lunch, dinner. Closed Mon

### TRISTAN (£££)

Serving *nouvelle cuisine* – expensive but widely considered the best restaurant on Mallorca.
✉ Puerto Portals marina ☎ 971 675547 🕐 Dinner only. Closed Mon except in summer

### WELLIES (££)

Waterside haunt of the jet set, where designer shorts are the norm. Good for steaks, fish, international food.
✉ Puerto Portals marina ☎ 971 683898 🕐 Lunch, dinner

## PORTO COLOM

### CELLER SA SINIA (££)

Seafood specialities in a perfect spot on the waterfront.
✉ Carrer des Pescadors ☎ 971 824323 🕐 Lunch, dinner. Closed Mon

## PUIGPUNYENT

### THE ROSE (££)

This long-established restaurant beside the church offers European and Spanish cooking.
✉ Carrer Galilea 24 ☎ 971 614180 🕐 Dinner only Wed–Sun

### SA TAFONA (£££)

Creative Balearic cuisine served in an old olive press at Mallorca's top country house hotel. The hotel also has Le Gazebo, a poolside barbecue, open in summer.
✉ Finca Son Net ☎ 971 147000 🕐 Lunch, dinner

## RANDA

### CELLER BAR RANDA (£)

Good-value Mallorcan cuisine in the village bar beside the church.

- ✉ Carrer Església 24
- ☎ 971 660989
- 🕐 Lunch, dinner. Closed Wed

### ES RECO DE RANDA (££)

Mallorcan and Spanish cooking in an old hotel at the foot of Puig de Randa.

- ✉ Carrer Fuente 13
- ☎ 971 660997
- 🕐 Lunch, dinner

## S'ARRACÓ

### LA TULIPE (££)

Modern European cooking in a New Age arty atmosphere.

- ✉ Plaça de Toledo 2 ☎ 971 671449 🕐 Dinner Mon–Sat

## SANTA MARIA DEL CAMÌ

### MOLI D'ES TORRENT (£££)

German chef Peter Himbert offers a personal interpretation of German and Mallorcan cuisine a this restaurant in an old windmill.

- ✉ Carretera Bunyola 75
- ☎ 971 140503 🕐 Lunch, dinner. Closed Thu

## SANT ELM

### EL PESCADOR (££)

Fish restaurant on the jetty with its own fishing boat and fine views of Sa Dragonera.

- ✉ Avinguda Jaume I
- ☎ 971 239198
- 🕐 Lunch, dinner

## SINEU

### CELLER SA FONT (££)

Traditional *celler* with wine vats lining the walls – very busy on market day.

- ✉ Plaça d'Espanya 18
- ☎ 971 520313
- 🕐 Lunch, dinner

## SÓLLER

### BENS D'AVALL (£££)

Creative Mediterranean cuisine in a fabulous setting with views of the northwest coast. Try the seven-course gourmet tasting menu.

- ✉ Carretera Deià–Sóller, Urbanización Costa de Deià
- ☎ 971 632381
- 🕐 Lunch, dinner Tue–Sun, Apr–Nov

### CA N'AI (££)

Fine food and elegant service on the terace of a country house hotel surrounded by orange groves.

- ✉ Camí Son Sales
- ☎ 971 632494 🕐 Feb–Oct, lunch, dinner. Closed Mon

### SA COVA (££)

Mallorcan classics (stuffed aubergines and rabbit with garlic) in a great position on Sóller's main square.

- ✉ Plaça Constitució 7
- ☎ 971 633222
- 🕐 Lunch, dinner. Closed Sun dinner and Mon

## VALLDEMOSSA

### CA'N COSTA (££)

Mallorcan and Spanish cuisine in a converted oil-mill.

- ✉ Carretera Valldemossa–Deià, km2.5 ☎ 971 612263
- 🕐 Lunch, dinner

### COFFEE AND LIQUEURS

In Spain, *un café* after the meal means only one thing: *café solo*, served short, strong and black, with sugar. Ask for a *carajillo* and it will have brandy added, or a bottle of *coñac* left on the table for you to help yourself. If the waiter brings a liqueur with your coffee, this is a *copa*, a treat on the house. Enjoy!

# In Palma

## PRICES

Prices are for a double room, excluding breakfast and VAT:

£ = under €60
££ = €60–€120
£££ = over €120

These prices will be much lower if you book as part of a package holiday. Most hotels in the main resorts are block-booked by tour operators and it is through them that you will get the cheapest deals.

## WHAT DOES IT MEAN?

All accommodation in Spain is strictly classified and graded by the government. Hotels are graded from one to five stars; *hostals*, with fewer facilities but often just as comfortable, from one star to three. A *hotel residencia* or *hostal residencia* is one that does not serve evening meals.

### ARABELLA SHERATON (£££)

One of the top hotels on the island, with all the expected luxuries. Near a golf course, 5km north of the city.

✉ Carrer de la Vinagrella, Son Vida ☎ 971 799999
🕐 All year

### BORN (££)

Two-star *hotel residencia* in a converted mansion near the Born. Good value if you want character in the old city.

✉ Carrer Sant Jaume 3
☎ 971 712942 🕐 All year

### CUITAT JARDI (£££)

One of Mallorca's earliest tourist hotels has reopened after major renovation. The Moorish-style building is behind the beach, with fabulous views of Palma, a 1-hour walk around the bay.

✉ Carrer Illa de Malta 14, Cuitat Jardi ☎ 971 260007
🕐 All year

### MELIÁ VICTORIA (£££)

Huge modern hotel which dominates the harbour. Most rooms have views of the cathedral and bay.

✉ Avinguda Joan Miró 21
☎ 971 732542 🕐 All year

### PALACIO CA SA GALESA (£££)

A beautifully restored 17th-century merchant's house between the cathedral and the Arab baths. There is a rooftop terrace and the only indoor pool to be found in the old city.

✉ Carrer de Miramar 8
☎ 971 715400 🕐 All year

### PALAU SA FONT (£££)

A 16th-century palace converted into a boutique hotel, with pink walls, wooden floors and a small terrace pool.

✉ Carrer dels Apuntadors 38
☎ 971 712277 🕐 All year

### PALLADIUM (££)

A good-value alternative choice a short walk from the city centre.

✉ Passeig de Mallorca 40
☎ 971 712841 🕐 All year

### PONS (£)

Simple one-star *hostal* in an old Palma house, with rooms arranged around a central courtyard.

✉ Carrer Vi 8
☎ 971 722658 🕐 All year

### RITZI (£)

Budget *hostal* centrally located for Palma's *tapas* bars and nightlife quarter.

✉ Carrer Apuntadors 6
☎ 971 714610 🕐 All year

### SAN LORENZO (££)

Six rooms only in a restored 17th-century manor house. Attractive garden with swimming pool close to the old city.

✉ Carrer Sant Llorenç 14
☎ 971 728200 🕐 All year

### SON VIDA (£££)

Exclusive hotel in a 13th-century castle with its own golf course. Open all year.

✉ Urbanización Son Vida Raixa 2 ☎ 971 790000

### VALPARAISO PALACE (£££)

Enjoy spectacular views over the Bay of Palma from this five-star hotel

✉ Carrer Francisco Vidal
☎ 971 400300 🕐 All year

# Around the Island

## ALGAIDER

### RAIMS (££)
Rural apartments around the courtyard of a 17th-century house whose owners produce their own wine.
- ✉ Carrer Ribera 21
- ☎ 971 665157 ● All year

## ARTÀ

### CA'N MORAGUES (££)
Just eight rooms and a heated swimming pool and sauna in this stylish renovated town house.
- ✉ Carrer Pou Nou 12
- ☎ 971 829509 ● All year

## BANYALBUFAR

### BARONIA (£)
Two-star *hostal* in a former mansion with courtyard, watchtower, swimming pool and sea views.
- ✉ Carrer Baronia 16
- ☎ 971 618146 ● Apr–Oct

### MAR I VENT (££)
Wonderful views from the terrace of this family-run hotel. Swimming pool and tennis court.
- ✉ Carrer Major 49
- ☎ 971 618000 ● Feb–Nov

## BINISSALEM

### SCOTT'S (£££)
Discreet British-run hotel in a 19th-century town house on the church square.
- ✉ Plaça Església 12
- ☎ 971 870100 ● All year

## CALA FIGUERA

### VILLA SERENA (£)
Simple two-star hotel, at the mouth of a pretty bay.
- ✉ Carrer Virgen del Carmen 37 ☎ 971 645303
- ● All year

## CALA D'OR

### CALA D'OR (££)
Ibizan-style hotel set among the pine trees overlooking the beach.
- ✉ Avinguda Bélgica 49
- ☎ 971 657249 ● Feb–Oct

## CALA RAJADA

### SES ROTGES (££)
An old-style villa with a garden, with a Michelin-starred restaurant.
- ✉ Carrer Rafael Blanes 21
- ☎ 971 563108
- ● Apr–Oct

## CALA SANT VICENÇ

### CALA SANT VICENÇ (£££)
This family-run seaside hotel near Pollença moved into the luxury bracket after a major renovation in 1996. Facilities include a sauna, gym and a heated outdoor pool.
- ✉ Carrer Maressers 2
- ☎ 971 530250
- ● Feb–Nov

## DEIÀ

### LA RESIDENCIA (£££)
A pair of 16th-century *fincas* with terraced orchards converted into a luxury hotel which is considered by many to be the best on the island. There are four-poster beds and teddy bears in every suite.
- ✉ Finca Son Canals
- ☎ 971 639011
- ● All year

## REIS DE MALLORCA

Reis de Mallorca (Kings of Mallorca) is an independent group of 18 Mallorcan hotels. It includes some of the best hotels on the island, like Palacio Ca Sa Galesa in Palma, Son Net in Puigpunyent and Ca's Puers in Sóller, but also cheaper options like the Costa d'Or in Lluc-Alcari and the Mar i Vent in Banyalbufar. What they all have in common is individuality, architectural beauty and generally excellent cuisine. Reis de Mallorca hotels can be booked on ☎ 971 770737 or visit www.reisdemallorca.com

# Around the Island

## MONASTERIES

Several of Mallorca's former monasteries rent out old monks' and pilgrims' cells to travellers. You may not get a shower but you will find peace, a sense of history and unforgettable hilltop views. The best known, at Lluc, is now virtually a hotel; for real solitude head instead for the Ermita de Bonany (► 52), Puig de Maria or the Santuari de Montesió at Porreres.

### S'HOTEL D'ES PUIG (££)

The 'hotel on the hill' as featured in a short story by Robert Graves and in Gordon West's *Jogging Round Majorca*.
✉ Carrer Es Puig 4
☎ 971 639409 ⏰ All year

## FORMENTOR

### HOTEL FORMENTOR (££££)

Mallorca's first luxury hotel outside Palma, opened in 1929. This is a grand hotel in a beautiful setting between the beach and the pine woods, with acres of terraced gardens.
✉ Platja de Formentor
☎ 971 899100
⏰ Apr–Oct and Christmas

## FORNALUTX

### CA'N VERDERA (£££)

An old stone house has been tastefully converted into a modern boutique hotel: relax among the orange groves.
✉ Carrer de Toros 1 ☎ 971 638203 ⏰ Mar–Oct

## INCA

### MONNABER NOU (££££)

A 13th-century manor house, set in oak and pine woods.
✉ Monnaber Nou, Campanet
☎ 971 877176 ⏰ All year

## LLUC

### MONESTIR DE LLUC (£)

Comfortable rooms in a former monastery – a good base for walking in the Serra de Tramuntana.
✉ Lluc monastery
☎ 971 871525 ⏰ All year

## LLUC-ALCARI

### COSTA D'OR (£)

Simple hotel in a magical setting above the sea; you can walk to the shore through the hotel's own pine forest.
✉ Lluc-Alcari
☎ 971 639025 ⏰ Apr–Oct

## LLUCMAJOR

### SON ANTEM (£££)

Luxury golf resort and spa hotel owned by the Marriott group, who are also building a timeshare village on the same site.
✉ Carretera Palma–Llucmajor
☎ 971 129100 ⏰ All year

## MANACOR

### LA RESERVA ROTANA (£££)

This 17th-century mansion with its own golf course is typical of Mallorca's new breed of upmarket rural hotels.
✉ Cami de S'Avall, km3
☎ 971 845685 ⏰ Feb–Nov

## ORIENT

### L'HERMITAGE (££)

A former convent turned into a country-house hotel, with swimming pool, tennis courts, sauna and a first-class restaurant.
✉ Carretera Alaró–Bunyola
☎ 971 180303
⏰ Feb–Nov

### HOSTAL MUNTANYA (££)

A former walkers' hostel recently renovated as part of the trend towards upmarket rural tourism.
✉ Carretera de Bunyola
☎ 971 615373 ⏰ All year

## POLLENÇA

### JUMA (££)

This early 20th-century hotel on the main square has recently reopened its doors to cater for the growing numbers of people wanting to stay in inland towns. Eight comfortable rooms decorated in antique style.

✉ Plaça Major 9 ☎ 971 535002 🕐 All year

## PORT DE POLLENÇA

### ILLA D'OR (££)

An old-fashioned hotel at the end of the promenade.

✉ Passeig Colón 265 ☎ 971 865100 🕐 Feb–Nov

## PORT DE SÓLLER

### ES PORT (£)

Three-star family-run *hostal* in a 15th-century mansion. The bar has the biggest olive press you'll ever see.

✉ Carrer Antoni Montis ☎ 971 631650 🕐 All year

## PUIG DE RANDA

### SANTUARI DE CURA (£)

Stay in rooms in an old monastery, with spectacular views from the terrace at dusk.

✉ Summit of Puig de Randa ☎ 971 120260 🕐 All year

## SANTA MARIA DEL CAMÍ

### READ'S (£££)

British-run hotel and sophisticated restaurant in a magnificent restored *finca* on the road to Alaró.

✉ Carretera Santa Maria– Alaró ☎ 971 140261 🕐 All year

## SES ILLETES

### BON SOL (£££)

Delightful family-run hotel, arranged like a wedding-cake on several levels and cascading down a hill to its own private beach.

✉ Passeig Illetes 30 ☎ 971 402111 🕐 Closed Nov

## SINEU

### LEON DE SINEU (££)

Small three-star hotel in a converted town house close to the main square.

✉ Carrer dels Bous 129 ☎ 971 520211 🕐 All year

## SÓLLER

### CA N'AI (£££)

Four-star *hotel rural* located in a manor house surrounded by orange groves.

✉ Camí Son Sales 50 ☎ 971 632494 🕐 Feb–Oct

### EL GUÍA (£)

This old-style hotel/ restaurant can be found by the station and is excellent value.

✉ Carrer Castanyer 2 ☎ 971 630227 🕐 Apr–Oct

## VALLDEMOSSA

### CA'N MARIO (£)

Charming family-run *hostal* filled with antiques. There is a good restaurant on the first floor.

✉ Carrer Uetam 8 ☎ 971 612122 🕐 All year

*FINCAS*

Many of Mallorca's *fincas* (country estates) have recently been converted into upmarket tourist accommodation, combining character (antiques and log fires) with modern amenities like swimming pools. Some, like Es Figueral Nou at Montuïri, have become hotels; others, like Sa Torre, on an old wine estate near Santa Eugènia, have been turned into apartments for rent. You can get information on *fincas* from the Associació Agroturisme Balear, Avinguda Gabriel Alomar Villalonga 8a, Palma (☎ 971 721508; www.agroturismo-balear.com) or from the independent association (www.fincaturismo.com).

# Markets

## WEEKLY MARKETS

Almost every town in Mallorca has a weekly market; most start early and wind up by lunchtime. The larger markets all follow a similar pattern – fresh produce around the main square, specialist food stalls fanning out from there, then cheap clothes, household goods and craft stalls for the tourists. The biggest market is on Thursdays at Inca; the most traditional is the Wednesday agricultural and livestock market at Sineu.

### PALMA

#### LLOTJA DEL PEIX (FISH MARKET)

Get here early as the night's catch goes on sale and mullet, prawns, sardines and sea bass are hawked by women with operatic voices.

✉ Es Moll de Pescadors
🕓 Mon–Sat 6AM

#### MERCAT ARTESANAL

This lively craft market on the Plaça Major also features buskers and open-air cafés.

✉ Plaça Major 🕓 Mon–Sat 10–2 in summer; Fri, Sat only in winter

#### MERCAT OLIVAR

Palma's main market, in a hall near Plaça d'Espanya. Fresh produce on the ground floor, meat and cheese upstairs, plus cheap *tapas* stalls.

✉ Plaça Olivar ☎ 971 720315 🕓 Mon–Sat 8–2

#### PERE GARAU

Local farmers bring their produce – including live animals – to this lively market in the east of the city.

✉ Plaça Pere Garau
🕓 Mon–Sat 7–2

#### RAMBLA

It may not match its Barcelona namesake, but Palma's Rambla is similarly lined with flower stalls.

✉ Passieg de la Rambla
🕓 Mon–Fri 8–2, 5–8, Sat 8–2

#### RASTRO (FLEA MARKET)

A Palma institution which takes over part of the main ring road each Saturday morning. Plenty of bargains but lots of junk too.

✉ Avinguda de Gabriel Alomar i Villalonga 🕓 Sat 8–2

#### SANTA CATALINA

A market for fresh fruit and vegetables – located just to the west of the city centre.

✉ Plaça Navegació
🕓 Mon–Sat 7–2

### WEEKLY MARKETS OUTSIDE PALMA

Alaró – *Fri*
Alcúdia – *Tue, Sun*
Algaida – *Fri*
Andratx – *Wed*
Artà – *Tue*
Binissalem – *Fri, Sun*
Cala Rajada – *Sat*
Calvià – *Mon*
Campos – *Thu, Sat*
Capdepera – *Wed*
Colònia de Sant Jordi – *Wed*
Felanitx – *Sun*
Inca – *Thu*
Llucmajor – *Wed, Sun*
Manacor – *Mon*
Montuïri – *Mon*
Muro – *Sun*
Petra – *Wed*
Pollença – *Sun*
Porreres – *Tue*
Port de Pollença – *Wed*
Porto Cristo – *Sun*
Pòrtol – *Thu*
Santa Eugènia – *Sat*
Santa Maria del Camí – *Sun*
Santanyí – *Wed, Sat*
S'Arenal – *Thu*
Ses Salines – *Thu*
Sineu – *Wed*
Sóller – *Sat*
Valldemossa – *Sun*
Vilafranca de Bonany – *Wed*

# Shopping in Palma

## SHOPPING DISTRICTS

The main shopping areas in Palma are Avinguda Jaume III for upmarket boutiques and the pedestrian streets around Plaça Major for small specialist shops. Centro Comercial Porto Pi, a modern shopping mall and hypermarket complex, is 2km from the centre.

## BOOKS

### LA CASA DEL MAPA
Books and maps about Mallorca.
- ✉ Carrer Sant Domingo 11
- ☎ 971 225944

### ERESO
Good selection of books about Mallorca in English and German.
- ✉ Carrer Paraires 1
- ☎ 971 710283

### FIOL
Palma's leading second-hand bookshop.
- ✉ Carrer Oms 45
- ☎ 971 721428

### FUNDACIÓ LA CAIXA
Art books and posters on the ground floor of this modern art gallery.
- ✉ Plaça Weyler 3  ☎ 971 728071  🕐 Mon–Sat 10–9, Sun 10–2

## DEPARTMENT STORES

### EL CORTE INGLÉS
Mallorca's two branches of Spain's leading department store. The Club del Gourmet has Spanish wines, hams and cheeses.
- ✉ Avinguda Jaume III 15; Avinguda Alexandre Rosselló 12
- ☎ 971 770177
- 🕐 Mon–Sat 10–10

## FOOD & WINE

### BONS VINS
Excellent selection of Mallorcan and Spanish wines and olive oils.
- ✉ Carrer Sant Feliu 7
- ☎ 971 214041

### COLMADO SANTO DOMINGO
Hundreds of hanging *sobrasada* sausages and cheeses, fig cake and oils.
- ✉ Carrer Sant Domingo 1
- ☎ 971 714887

### FORN D'ES TEATRE
Art nouveau shopfront, and a good place to buy *ensaimadas*.
- ✉ Plaça Weyler 9
- ☎ 971 715254

### FORN FONDO
This bakery has been turning out *ensaimadas* since 1911.
- ✉ Carrer Unió 15
- ☎ 971 711634

### FRASQUET
Go in here just to smell the melted chocolate.
- ✉ Carrer Brossa 19
- ☎ 971 721354

### LA MONTAÑA
Sausages, hams, cheeses and one of Palma's best window displays.
- ✉ Carrer Jaume II 27
- ☎ 971 712595

### SON VIVOT
Mallorcan and Menorcan produce.
- ✉ Plaça Porta Pintada 1
- ☎ 971 720748

## SHOPPING TIPS

Most shops are open from around 10 to 1:30 and 5 to 8 Monday to Friday, and on Saturday mornings. The exceptions are souvenir shops in the large resorts, which stay open every day, and the Gigante chain of supermarkets, open throughout the day Monday to Saturday. Larger shops accept credit cards and travellers' cheques, but it is always advisable to have some cash.

# Arts and Crafts in Palma

## SIURELLS

*Siurells* are clay whistles, which have been made on Mallorca since Arab times. They come in all shapes and sizes – the most common design is a man on horseback – and are painted white with flashes of red and green. They are cheap, children love them, and the artist Joan Miró was much influenced by their brightness and simplicity.

### ALPARGATERÍA LLINAS
The best place to buy espadrilles.
- ✉ Carrer Sant Miquel 43
- ☎ 971 717696

### ARTESANIES POL
A good selection of ceramics and glass, centrally situated near the top of the Born.
- ✉ Carrer Unió 13
- ☎ 971 724299

### LA CASA DEL OLIVO
Wonderful olive-carver's workshop in an alley off Carrer Jaume II. The best buy here is salad bowls – they're not cheap but you're paying for the quality and old-fashioned craftsmanship.
- ✉ Carrer Pescatería Vella 4
- ☎ 971 727025

### CENTRO PELAIRES
Wander through the back streets of Palma and you come across numerous contemporary art galleries. This is one of the best, featuring work by Mallorcan and international artists.
- ✉ Carrer Verí 3
- ☎ 971 720375

### FANG I FOC
This shop stocks a good range of ceramics from Mallorca and the Spanish mainland.
- ✉ Carrer Libertat 29
- ☎ 971 455860

### FET A MÀ
As the name implies, everything is 'made by hand'. Pottery and glass are on sale, in traditional and modern style.
- ✉ Carrer Sant Miquel 52
- ☎ 971 711095

### HERREROS DE VICENTE JUAN RIBAS
The best place in Palma to buy *roba de llengues* patterned cloth.
- ✉ Carrer Sant Nicolau 10
- ☎ 971 721773

### MAJÓRICA
Palma branch of Mallorca's leading artificial-pearl-maker.
- ✉ Avinguda Jaume III 11
- ☎ 971 725268/722919

### MIDGE DALTON
Palma's antique shops are perfect for browsing, and this is one of the best.
- ✉ Plaça Mercat 20
- ☎ 971 713360

### NATURA
Mallorcan branch of a Spanish chain selling eco-friendly gifts.
- ✉ Passeig des Born 9
- ☎ 971 718252

### ORQUÍDEA
Cultured pearls – slightly cheaper than its rival Majórica.
- ✉ Plaça Rei Joan Carles I
- ☎ 971 715797

### PERSÉPOLIS
High-class antiques on Palma's upmarket shopping street.
- ✉ Avinguda Jaume III 23
- ☎ 971 724539

### S'AVARCA
Traditional Menorcan handmade sandals.
- ✉ Costa de Sant Domingo 14
- ☎ 971 712058

### VIDRIERÍAS GORDIOLA
The best choice of Algaida glassware in Palma.
- ✉ Carrer Victoria 2
- ☎ 971 711541

# Arts and Crafts Around the Island

## ALGAIDA

### VIDRIERÍAS GORDIOLA
Glass factory and museum
(► 59) in a mock castle.
- ✉ Carretera Palma–Manacor,
km19 ☎ 971 665046

## INCA

### MUNPER
Mallorcan leather is rarely
a bargain, but come here
for a wide selection of
shoes, handbags and belts.
- ✉ Carretera Palma–Alcúdia,
km30 ☎ 971 881000

## LLUCMAJOR

### CASA ORDINAS
Master cutler producing
old-fashioned knives and
tools at very good prices.
- ✉ Carrer Vall 128
- ☎ 971 660580

## MANACOR

### MAJÓRICA
Shop here after touring
Mallorca's largest pearl
factory (► 59).
- ✉ Avinguda Majórica 48
- ☎ 971 550200

### OLIVART
Everything here is made
from olive wood.
- ✉ Carretera Palma–Manacor,
km45 ☎ 971 552800

## MONTUÏRI

### ORQUÍDEA
Large factory shop
featuring artificial pearls.
- ✉ Carretera Palma–Manacor,
km30 ☎ 971 644144

## PÒRTOL

### CA'S CANONGE
Large selection of pottery,
especially heavy brown-
glazed cooking pots.
- ✉ Carrer Trinitat 61
- ☎ 971 602361

### CA'N VENT
Traditional Mallorcan
pottery – the first of two
good ollerías in this street.
- ✉ Carrer Trinitat 39
- ☎ 971 602456

### ROCA LLISA
One of the best places to
buy siurells (► 76).
- ✉ Carrer Roca Llisa 26
- ☎ 971 602497

## SANTA MARIA DEL CAMÍ

### CA'N BERNAT
Master craftsman's
workshop turning out
imaginative local pottery.
- ✉ Carrer Bartomeu Pasqual
- ☎ 971 621306

## SANTANYÍ

### CERAMIQUES DE SANTANYÍ
Innovative ceramic
designs, based on ancient
Mallorcan traditions.
- ✉ Carrer Guardia Civil 22
- ☎ 971 163128

## SÓLLER

### EUGENIO
Gifts carved out of olive
wood – salad bowls, salt-
cellars, chess sets.
- ✉ Carrer Jerónimo Estades
11A ☎ 971 630984

### FET A SÓLLER
Shop in the station selling
local produce and crafts.
Profits go to a workshop
for those with disabilities.
- ✉ Estació de Sóller
- ☎ 971 633942

### CRAFT FAIRS
A *Fira del Fang* (Ceramics
Fair) is held each March in the
town of Marratxí and all of
Mallorca's leading potters are
represented. Prices here are
much better than in the tourist
shops. *Baleart* is a Christmas
craft fair held in Palma each
December, with stalls selling
everything from pottery and
handmade shoes to Mallorcan
wines and *sobrasada*
sausages.

# Theatres and Concerts

## WHAT'S ON?

To find out what's on while you are staying, ask any tourist office for a copy of *Where To Go*, published quarterly in English and German. The *Majorca Daily Bulletin* also has daily listings. A monthly guide to events in Palma is published in Spanish and Catalan and available at tourist offices and hotels. Remember that everything starts late in Mallorca – opera at 9PM, theatre around 10PM and music any time up to midnight.

## COSTA NORD

The American actor Michael Douglas could be seen as a 21st-century successor to Archduke Ludwig Salvator, using his money and his influence to promote the landscapes and culture of Mallorca. In 2000 he opened Costa Nord, a multimedia cultural centre in Valldemossa devoted to Mallorca's north coast. The visit begins with a short film, narrated by Douglas; it continues with a recreation of the Archduke's yacht, the *Nixe*, accompanied by a commentary on his Mediterranean voyages. The shop sells a range of pricey souvenirs; there is also a concert hall which attracts top international names during the Mediterranean Nights festival each summer.
✉ Avinguda Palma 6
☎ 971 616070

### PALMA

**AUDITÒRIUM**
This is Palma's main venue for theatre and concerts.
✉ Passeig Marítim 18
☎ 971 734735

**CASTELL DE BELLVER**
A venue for outdoor classical concerts on summer evenings.
✉ Parc Bellver
☎ 971 287565

**PARC DE LA MAR**
Free concerts (jazz, rock or classical) beneath the city walls in summer.
✉ Parc de la Mar

**TEATRE MUNICIPAL**
Contemporary drama, dance and ballet are all staged here, as well as film screenings.
✉ Passeig Mallorca 9
☎ 971 739148

**TEATRE PRINCIPAL**
Nineteenth-century theatre with autumn and spring opera seasons.
✉ Plaça Weyler 7
☎ 971 725548

### ALCÚDIA

**AUDITORI D'ALCÚDIA**
A stunning new hall hosting concerts and drama.
✉ Plaça de la Porta de Mallorca
☎ 971 897185

### CALA MILLOR

**SA MÀNIGA**
New auditorium with regular concerts and exhibitions.
✉ Carrer Son Galta 4
☎ 971 587373

### CALA RAJADA

**JARDINS CASA MARCH**
The gardens and sculpture park provide a pretty setting for a series of evening concerts in July.
✉ Parc Casa March
☎ 971 563033

### DEIÀ

**SON MARROIG**
Concerts are staged on summer evenings in the gardens created by Archduke Ludwig Salvator. Deià's annual classical music festival is held here.
✉ Carretera Valldemossa–Deià ☎ 971 639178

### ESPORLES

**LA GRANJA**
Displays of folk music and dancing on Wednesday and Friday afternoons.
✉ La Granja
☎ 971 610032

### POLLENÇA

**CONVENT SANT DOMINGO**
Pollença's annual music festival is held in the cloisters of this 17th-century monastery.
✉ Carrer Sant Domingo
☎ 971 534012

### VALLDEMOSSA

**REIAL CARTOIXA**
The Chopin festival is held each August in the town's Carthusian monastery.
✉ Valldemossa
☎ 971 612351

# Bars

## RESORT BARS

Bars in the main resorts
change their names and
identities so frequently
that recommendations are
useless – follow your nose
and you will soon find one
that you like. Many bars
are foreign-owned, with
German or British names,
imported beer and
satellite TV. A stretch of
the Platja de Palma is
known as *carrer de la
cervesa* ('Beer Street')
owing to the number of
German bars; the British
equivalent is in Magaluf.

### PALMA

The best places for late-
night bar-hopping are in
the streets around Plaça
de la Llotja and the
terrace bars along the
waterfront on Passeig
Marítim.

### BARCELONA
Cool jazz bar in a
basement beside Abaco.
✉ Carrer Apuntadors 5 ☎
971 713557 🕐 From 9PM; live
jazz from midnight nightly

### LA BODEGUITA DEL
### MEDIO
Enjoy Cuban food, rum
and *salsa* music – an
imitation of its Havana
namesake. Go late.
✉ Carrer Vallseca 18 ☎
971 717832 🕐 From 10PM

### CAPPUCCINO GRAND
### CAFÉ
The hippest meeting
place in town in an old
Renaissance palace with a
shady courtyard and art
gallery.
✉ Carrer San Miquel 53 ☎
971 719764 🕐 8AM–1AM

### CAPPUCCINO GRAND
### CAFÉ
The original Café, on the
waterfront, is still a
popular place to meet for
coffee or cocktails.
✉ Passeig Marítim 1
☎ 971 282162
🕐 8:30AM–3AM

### HOGANS
Palma's first Irish pub
opened in 1996.
Occasional Irish fiddling,
popular with locals.
✉ Carrer Monsenyor Palmer 2
☎ 971 289664
🕐 12 noon–3AM

### MADE IN BRASIL
A popular meeting-
place for late-night
cocktails, smooching and
Latin dance.
✉ Passeig Marítim 27
☎ 670 372390 🕐 daily
8PM–4AM

### EL PESQUERO
Former fishermen's bar,
now a chic waterfront café
with *tapas*, drinks and
harbour views.
✉ Moll de la Llotja 2 ☎
971 721079 🕐 7:30AM–late

### VARADERO
Trendy terrace bar at the
end of the old quay, with
great views of the floodlit
cathedral.
✉ Moll Vell ☎ 971 726428
🕐 9AM–late

### NEAR PALMA

### ABACANTO
A cousin of Abaco (see
panel) in a 19th-century
mansion on an industrial
estate. It is quite difficult
to find, so take a taxi.
✉ Camí Son Nicolau,
S'Indioteria ☎ 971 430624

### ABACO

Palma's most unusual bar is
located in a 17th-century
palace close to La Llotja. Push
open a heavy wooden door in
the busy nightlife quarter and
you enter a different world.
Huge baskets of fruit cascade
onto the floor; there are fresh
flowers everywhere, and a
subtle hint of incense. You sip
fruit cocktails by candlelight,
while listening to classical
music, then wander into the
courtyard with its fountains
and caged birds. The drinks
are expensive, but everyone
should go once.
✉ Carrer Sant Joan 1
☎ 971 715974 🕐 7PM–2AM

7

# Discos and Dinner Shows

## DINNER SHOWS

A recent arrival in Mallorca is the 'themed' dinner show and spectacle, which can be anything from folklore and flamenco dancing to a medieval banquet complete with jousting and serving wenches. These shows are basically aimed at tour groups; you can book at any resort hotel. Don't go unless you are prepared to abandon your inhibitions and join in the fun.

## DISCOS

### PALMA

### IB'S
Palma's latest disco is situated directly beneath the seafront promenade.
- ✉ Passeig Marítim
- ☎ 971 733671
- ⏰ 11PM–6AM, nightly in summer; Thu–Sat in winter

### PACHA
A branch of one of the most famous club chains, Pacha is for those in search of a serious night out.
- ✉ Passeig Marítim 42
- ☎ 971 455908 ⏰ 10PM to late; nightly in summer; Thu–Sat in winter

### TITO'S
Not quite as young as nearby Pacha (▶ above). There are six bars, a laser show and fantastic views over Palma bay. You enter via an outdoor lift from the seafront promenade.
- ✉ Passeig Marítim
- ☎ 971 730017
- ⏰ 11PM–6PM; nightly in summer; Thu–Sat in winter

### AROUND THE ISLAND

### BCM
This is the largest and probably the loudest disco in Europe, with laser shows, banks of video screens, a swimming pool and room for 4,000 people. The upper level is dedicated to the young-and-trendy crowd, while the over-30s gather downstairs. Big-name international stars are featured in live shows

here throughout the summer season.
- ✉ Avinguda S'Olivera, Magaluf ☎ 971 131546
- ⏰ 10PM–5AM; nightly in summer, weekends in winter

### JOY
Loud, brash, late-night disco with regular summer visits from some big-name DJs.
- ✉ Carrer de la Missió de Sant Gabriel, Platja de Palma ☎ 971 262007 ⏰ 11PM–6AM nightly in summer

### MENTA
Designed like a Roman temple around an open-air pool, it honours Alcúdia's history each May with a 'Roman orgy'.
- ✉ Avinguda Argentina, Port d'Alcúdia ☎ 971 891972
- ⏰ 11PM–6AM, nightly in summer; weekends only in winter

## DINNER SHOWS

### AROUND THE ISLAND

### CASINO MALLORCA
A choice of gambling in the casino (passport and smart dress required) or the Paladium dinner show with dancing.
- ✉ Urbanización Sol de Mallorca, Magaluf ☎ 971 454508 ⏰ Casino 8PM–5AM nightly; show Tue, Thu, Sat 10PM

### PIRATE ADVENTURE
Yo-ho-ho and a bundle of fun on a mock pirate ship – with plenty of audience participation required. Don't say you weren't warned!
- ✉ Carretera La Porrassa, Magaluf ☎ 971 130411
- ⏰ Times vary

# Golf Courses

## PALMA

**SON VIDA**
Mallorca's first golf course, opened in 1964 on an exclusive estate above Palma. A second course, Son Muntaner, has now opened on the same site.
✉ Urbanización Son Vida
☎ 971 791210

## BUNYOLA

**SON TERMENS**
Attractive course on an old hunting estate.
✉ Carrer de S'Esglaieta, km10
☎ 971 617862

## CALA MILLOR

**SON SERVERA**
Nine-hole course amid pine woods by the sea.
✉ Urbanización Costa dels Pins, 6km from Cala Millor
☎ 971 840096

## CAMP DE MAR

**GOLF DE ANDRATX**
A challenging course with narrow fairways, lakes and sea views.
✉ Carretera Camp de Mar
☎ 971 236280

## CAPDEPERA

**CANYAMEL**
A testing course – small greens, sloping fairways and sea breezes.
✉ Urbanización Canyamel
☎ 971 841313

**PULA GOLF**
Challenging course on a luxury resort between Cala Millor and Capdepera.
✉ Carretera Son Servera–Capdepera, km3 ☎ 971 817034

## LLUCMAJOR

**SON ANTEM**
Wide fairways, fast greens and hidden water hazards.
✉ 3km outside Llucmajor on the PM602 to Palma
☎ 971 661124

## MAGALUF

**PONIENTE**
A long and difficult 18-hole course.
✉ Carretera Cala Figuera
☎ 971 130148

## POLLENÇA

**POLLENSA**
A tight 9-hole course, with small greens and narrow fairways on a hill with views out to sea.
✉ 2km outside Pollença on Palma road ☎ 971 533216

## PORTO COLOM

**VALL D'OR**
Set among pine trees close to the east coast.
✉ Carretera Porto Colom–Cala d'Or ☎ 971 837068

## SANTA PONÇA

**SANTA PONÇA**
This is the venue for the Balearic Open: long, wide fairways set in the midst of open countryside.
✉ Urbanización Golf Santa Ponça ☎ 971 690211

## SES ILLETES

**REAL GOLF DE BENDINAT**
Undulating course set among pine woods above the bay of Palma.
✉ Urbanización Bendinat
☎ 971 405200

**GOLF IN MALLORCA**

In 1976 there were two golf courses in Mallorca; now there are 15 and more are being built. All are open throughout the year, providing a refuge for golfers fleeing frost and winter greens elsewhere. The typical cost of a round is €50–€60, though this is much reduced if you come on a golfing package holiday. Don't forget to bring a handicap certificate.

# Watersports

## SAILING IN MALLORCA

Mallorca has 41 marinas, 30 *clubs nautics* and mooring for 10,000 yachts. Yachts can be chartered locally and most marinas also have facilities for water-skiing and windsurfing. Highlights of the sailing year include the King's Cup in August, the Princess Sofía trophy at Easter, and the Rei en Jaume regatta in July when a flotilla of yachts re-creates the 185km journey made by Jaume the Conqueror when he landed at Santa Ponça in 1229.

## WINDSURFING

There are schools at several of the larger resorts and it is also possible to hire equipment without tuition. Beaches where windsurfing is available include Cala Millor, Cala d'Or, Can Picafort, Formentor, Magaluf, Palma Nova, Peguera, Platja de Palma, Port d'Alcúdia, Port de Pollença, Portals Nous and Santa Ponça.

## SAILING

### BALEARES YACHT CHARTER

Ring for information on how to charter a boat. Boats are available with or without a crew.
☎ 971 727986

### ESCUELA NACIONAL DE VELA CALANOVA

The national sailing school in Cala Major runs courses and is also willing to offer advice on all aspects of sailing in and around Mallorca.
✉ Avinguda Joan Miró, Cala Major ☎ 971 402512

### SAIL AND SURF POLLENÇA

This prestigious sailing club and school is located on the northeast coast. Instruction is available both for beginners and for those more experienced.
✉ Passeig Saralegui 134, Port de Pollença ☎ 971 865346

### CALA D'OR MARINA
☎ 971 657070

### PORT D'ANDRATX MARINA
☎ 971 671721

### PORT DE POLLENÇA MARINA
☎ 971 864635

### PORTO COLOM MARINA
☎ 971 824658

### PORTO CRISTO MARINA
☎ 971 821253

### PUERTO PORTALS MARINA (PORTALS NOUS)
☎ 971 171100

### REIAL CLUB NAUTIC DE PALMA
☎ 971 726848

## SCUBA DIVING

### FEDERACIÓ BALEAR DE ACTIVIDADES SUBACUÁTICAS

The clear waters around the island of Mallorca are the perfect place for diving, especially in the small, shallow coves of the south and east coasts. The federation can give you information and advice on all aspects of diving, therefore, it is a good starting point.
✉ Carrer Pere d'Alcàntara Penya 13, Palma ☎ 971 463315

### ALBATROS
✉ Port Cala Bona, Cala Millor ☎ 971 586807

### AQUA MARINE DIVING
✉ Port d'Andratx ☎ 971 674376

### OCTOPUS
✉ Port de Sóller ☎ 971 633133

### SCUBA ACTIVA
✉ Sant Elm ☎ 971 239102

### UNIDAD COSTA NORTE
✉ Port Adriano, El Toro, Calvià ☎ 971 232676

## WATER-SKIING

Water-skiing equipment can be hired on all the most popular beaches, including Cala Millor, Can Picafort, Formentor, Magaluf, Palma Nova, Peguera, Platja de Palma, Port d'Alcúdia and Santa Ponça.

# Spectator Sports

## BULLFIGHTING

Bullfighting is considered an art form as much as a sport – a legacy from pagan rites. The leading *matadors* are national celebrities and there are fights most days on TV. A bullfight begins with a horseback procession, or *corrida*, followed by the fight itself; the bull is softened up by *picadores* and then the *matador* moves in for the kill. Many foreigners may detest the spectacle – but it is undoubtedly an important aspect of Spanish culture.

### PALMA

**PLAÇA DE TOROS**
Bullfights are held in this 1929 bullring between March and October. Choose between a seat in the sun (*sol*) or the shade (*sombra*).
✉ Avinguda Gaspar Bennazar Arquitecte ☎ 971 755245

### AROUND THE ISLAND

**PLAÇA DE TOROS, ALCÚDIA**
☎ 971 547903

**PLAÇA DE TOROS, FELANITX**
☎ 971 580557

**PLAÇA DE TOROS, INCA**
☎ 971 540087

**PLAÇA DE TOROS, MURO**
This bullring was built in 1910 inside its own quarry of white stone.
☎ 971 537 329

## CRICKET

### AROUND THE ISLAND

**MAGALUF CRICKET CLUB**
Cricket has been kept going by a group of British ex-patriates, who play local and visiting sides on their ground in Magaluf.
☎ 971 233262

## FOOTBALL

### PALMA

**SON MOIX**
The home of Real Mallorca FC, who play in the first division and reached the final of the European Cup Winners Cup in 1999. Matches on alternate Sunday afternoons, September to June.
✉ Camí dels Reis
☎ 971 221221

## HORSE-RACING

### PALMA

**HIPÓDROMO SON PARDO**
Europe's first floodlit racecourse opened in 1965. Trotting races (*carreras*) are held around a 1km track at 4:30 on Sundays in winter and 9PM on Fridays in summer. The jockey sits in a small cart behind the horse and must prevent the horse from breaking into a gallop. Trotting has been popular in Mallorca and Menorca for at least 200 years.
✉ Carretera Palma–Sóller, km3 ☎ 971 754031

## *TIRO CON HONDA (SLINGSHOT)*

The Roman historian Livy wrote of Balearic slingshot throwers being employed as mercenaries during Hannibal's crossing of the Alps in 218 BC; a statue of a Balearic slinger in the S'Hort del Rei gardens in Palma is a tribute to their importance in Mallorcan history. The art of the slingshot has recently been revived; to see today's slingers, contact the Club de Honderos,
✉ Bar España, Carrer Oms 31, Palma ☎ 971 726250.

# MALLORCA
*practical matters*

SOUPE
SALAD   TOMAT
SALAD   MIXED
SALAD   TUNA

TOAST   HAWAI
HAMBURGER   FRITES
OMMELETTE   HAM.CHEESE                    FRITES
OMMELETTE   CHAMPIGNONS
SPAGHETTI
HAM   SERRANO
GAMBAS   COCKTAIL   100 GR
CALAMARES   ROMANA
FISCH   FILET   FRITES
SALMON   TOAST   100 GR
SEEZUNGE   FRITES
SEEZUNGE   FILET   FRITES
GAMBAS   GRILL
MIXED   FISCH   GRILL
LAMB   KOTELETTEN   FRITES
2   KOTELETTEN   FRITES
1/2   CHICKEN   FRITES
CHICKEN   FILLET   CURRY   FRITES
WIENER   ESCALOPE   FRITES
JAEGER   ESCALOPE   FRITES
STEAK   FRITES

T.BONE
PAELLA   MIN 2 PERS

## WHAT YOU NEED

| ● Required ○ Suggested ▲ Not required | Some countries require a passport to remain valid for a minimum period (usually at least six months) beyond the date of entry – contact their consulate or embassy or your travel agent for details. | UK | Germany | USA | Netherlands | Spain |
|---|---|---|---|---|---|---|
| Passport/National Identity Card | | ● | ● | ● | ● | ▲ |
| Visa | | ▲ | ▲ | ▲ | ▲ | ▲ |
| Onward or Return Ticket | | ○ | ○ | ● | ○ | ○ |
| Health Inoculations | | ▲ | ▲ | ▲ | ▲ | ▲ |
| Health Documentation (➤ 90, Health) | | ● | ● | ● | ● | ▲ |
| Travel Insurance | | ● | ● | ● | ● | ▲ |
| Driving Licence (national with Spanish translation or International) | | ○ | ○ | ○ | ○ | ○ |
| Car Insurance Certificate | | ● | ● | ● | ● | ● |
| Car Registration Document | | ● | ● | ● | ● | ○ |

## WHEN TO GO

**Palma**

High season

Low season

| 14°C JAN | 15°C FEB | 17°C MAR | 19°C APR | 22°C MAY | 26°C JUN | 29°C JUL | 29°C AUG | 27°C SEP | 23°C OCT | 18°C NOV | 15°C DEC |
|---|---|---|---|---|---|---|---|---|---|---|---|

☁ Cloud  🌧 Wet  ☀ Sun  🌤 Sunshine/Showers

## TIME DIFFERENCES

| GMT 12 noon | Mallorca 1PM | Germany 1PM | USA (NY) 7AM | Netherlands 1PM | Rest of Spain 1PM |
|---|---|---|---|---|---|

## TOURIST OFFICES

**In the UK**
Spanish Tourist Office
22–23 Manchester Square
London W1M 5AP
☎ 020 7486 8077
Fax: 020 7486 8034

**In the USA**
Tourist Office of Spain
35th Floor, 665 Fifth Avenue
New York
NY 10103
☎ 212/265 8822
Fax: 212/265 8864

Tourist Office of Spain
8383 Wilshire Boulevard
Suite 960
Beverly Hills
CA 90211
☎ 323/658 7188
Fax: 323/658 1061

### ARRIVING

Spain's national airline, Iberia, has scheduled flights to Palma's Son Sant Joan Airport from major Spanish and European cities, but charter flights are much cheaper. Ferry services operate from the Spanish mainland, Menorca and Ibiza to Palma.

| **Son Sant Joan Airport** Kilometres to city centre | Journey times | |
|---|---|---|
| | 🚌 | N/A |
| **11 kilometres** | 🚆 | 30 minutes |
| | 🚍 | 15 minutes |

| **Palma Ferry Terminal** Kilometres to city centre | Journey times | |
|---|---|---|
| | 🚌 | N/A |
| **4 kilometres** | 🚆 | 30 minutes |
| | 🚍 | 10 minutes |

### MONEY

The euro is the official currency of Spain. Euro banknotes and coins were introduced in January 2002. Spain's former currency, the peseta, went out of circulation in early 2002.

Banknotes are in denominations of 5, 10, 20, 50, 100, 200 and 500 euros; coins are in denominations of 1, 2, 5, 10, 20 and 50 cents, and 1 and 2 euros.

Euro traveller's cheques are widely accepted, as are major credit cards. Credit and debit cards can also be used for withdrawing euro notes from ATMs. Banks can be found in most towns in Mallorca.

### TIME

 Like the rest of Spain, Mallorca is one hour ahead of Greenwich Mean Time (GMT+1), but from late March until late September, summer time (GMT+2) operates.

### CUSTOMS

 **You may bring goods such as cigarettes and spirits into Mallorca, from an EU country, for personal use, within these guidelines:**
800 cigarettes, 200 cigars, 1kilogram of tobacco
10 litres of spirits (+22%)
20 litres of aperitifs
90 litres of wine, of which 60 litres can be sparkling wine
110 litres of beer

**If you are bringing goods into Mallorca from a non-EU country for your personal use, the allowances are:**
200 cigarettes OR 50 cigars OR 250 grams of tobacco
1 litre of spirits (+22%)
2 litres of intermediary products (e.g. sherry) and sparkling wine
2 litres of still wine
50 grams of perfume
0.25 litres of eau de toilette
The value limit for goods is 175 euros.

**Travellers under 17 years of age are not entitled to the tobacco and alcohol allowance.**

➖ **NO**
Drugs, firearms, ammunition, offensive weapons, obscene material, unlicensed animals.

### CONSULATES

**UK**
☎ 971 712445

**Germany**
☎ 971 722371

**USA**
☎ 971 722660

**Netherlands**
☎ 971 716493

## WHEN YOU ARE THERE

### TOURIST OFFICES

**Mallorca Tourist Board**

● Fomento del Turismo de Mallorca
Carrer de Constitució 1
Palma 07001
☎ 971 725396

**Local Tourist Offices
(Oficinas de Información
Turística – OIT)**

**Palma**

● Carrer de Sant Domingo 11
Palma 07001
☎ 971 724090

● Parc de les Estacions
Palma 07002
☎ 971 754329

**Palma Nova**

● Passeig de la Mar 13
Calvià 07181
☎ 971 682365

**Port d'Alcúdia**

● Carretera Artà 68
Alcúdia 07410
☎ 971 892615

**Port de Pollença**

● Carrer de les Monges 9
Pollença 07470
☎ 971 865467

**Sóller**

● Plaça de Sa Constitució 1
Sóller 07100
☎ 971 630200

Other offices include: Cala d'Or, Cala Millor, Cala Rajada, Cala Sant Vicenç, Ca'n Picafort, Colònia de Sant Jordi, Magaluf, Peguera, Platja de Muro, Port de Sóller, Porto Cristo, S'Arenal, Ses Illetes, and Santa Ponça.

### NATIONAL HOLIDAYS

| J | F | M | A | M | J | J | A | S | O | N | D |
|---|---|---|---|---|---|---|---|---|---|---|---|
| 2 |   | (2) | (2) | 1 |   |   | 1 |   | 1 | 1 | 3 |

| | |
|---|---|
| 1 Jan | New Year's Day |
| 6 Jan | Epiphany |
| Mar/Apr | Good Friday, Easter Monday |
| 1 May | Labour Day |
| 15 Aug | Assumption of the Virgin |
| 12 Oct | National Day |
| 1 Nov | All Saints' Day |
| 6 Dec | Constitution Day |
| 8 Dec | Feast of the Immaculate Conception |
| 25 Dec | Christmas Day |

Many shops and offices close for longer periods around Christmas and Easter, as well as for the festivals of Corpus Christi in May/June and Sant Jaume on 25 July.

### OPENING HOURS

| ○ Shops | ● Churches |
|---|---|
| ● Offices | ● Museums |
| ● Banks | ● Pharmacies |

| 9 AM | 10 AM | 11 AM | 12 PM | 1 PM | 2 PM | 3 PM | 4 PM | 5 PM | 6 PM |
|---|---|---|---|---|---|---|---|---|---|
| 9:30 | 10:30 | 11:30 | 12:30 | 1:30 | 2:30 | 3:30 | 4:30 | 5:30 | |

In addition to the times shown above, large department stores, as well as supermarkets and shops in tourist resorts, may open outside these times, especially in summer. In general, pharmacies, banks and shops close on Saturday afternoon, though banks stay open until 4:30PM Monday to Thursday, October to May, but close Saturday, June to September.
The opening times of museums is just a rough guide; some are open longer hours in summer while hours are reduced in winter. Some museums close at weekends or another day in the week.

### ELECTRICITY

The power supply in Mallorca is: 220–225 volts.

Sockets accept two-pin plugs (round-pin style), so an adaptor is needed for most non-Continental appliances and a transformer for appliances operating on 100–120 volts.

### TIPS/GRATUITIES

| Yes ✓ | No ✗ | | |
|---|---|---|---|
| Restaurants (if service not included) | | ✓ | 10% |
| Cafés/bars (if service not included) | | ✓ | change |
| Tour guides | | ✓ | 1 euro |
| Hairdressers | | ✓ | change |
| Taxis | | ✓ | 10% |
| Chambermaids | | ✓ | 1 euro |
| Porters | | ✓ | 1 euro |
| Theatre/cinema usherettes | | ✓ | change |
| Cloakroom attendants | | ✓ | change |
| Toilets | | ✗ | |

## PUBLIC TRANSPORT

**Trains**
The main railway line connects Palma to Inca and Sa Pobla, with stops at Santa Maria del Camí, Binissalem and Muro. There are regular trains throughout the day, taking 35 minutes to Inca and 55 minutes to Sa Pobla (☎ 971 752245). Five trains a day leave for Palma for Sóller, beginning at 8AM (☎ 971 752051) and connecting with the tram to Port de Sóller (➤ 55). The two railway stations are found close together, beside Plaça d'Espanya.

**Island Buses**
A comprehensive network of buses connects Palma to Mallorca's main towns, with extra services linking the beach resorts in summer. Buses out of Palma depart from the new bus station on Carrer Eusebi Estada, behind Plaça d'Espanya. Palma has its own network of city buses, which also covers the beach resorts around Palma Bay (☎ 971 431024). Bus No. 25 is an express link between Plaça d'Espanya and the airport.

**Boat Trips**
In summer there are regular boat tours of Palma Bay and excursions from resorts including Cala d'Or, Port de Pollença and Port de Sóller. Some of these go to remote beaches which can only be reached by boat. One trip which runs throughout the year is the journey around the northwest coast from Port de Sóller to Sa Colobra (☎ 971 633109).

**Menorca** Day trips to Menorca can be made on a fast catamaran, which leaves Cala Rajada at 9AM daily, arriving at the Menorcan city of Ciutadella in one hour. The return journey leaves Ciutadella at 7:30PM (Cape Balear ☎ 902 100444). There are also daily car ferries to Ciutadella from Port d'Alcúdia (☎ 902 119128).

## CAR RENTAL

The leading international car rental companies have offices at Palma airport and you can book a car in advance (essential in peak periods) either direct or through a travel agent. Local companies offer competitive rates and will usually deliver a car to the airport.

## TAXIS

Taxis can be hired at ranks (indicated by a blue square with a 'T'), on the street (by flagging down those with a green light), or at hotels. They are good value within Palma but expensive over long distances. A list of tariffs is displayed at taxi ranks.

## CONCESSIONS

**Students** Holders of an International Student Identity Card may be able to obtain some concessions on travel, entrance fees etc, but Mallorca is not really geared up for students, it is more suited to families and senior citizens. However, there are two youth hostels on the island, one near Palma and the other outside Alcúdia. Another cheap form of accommodation is to stay in a monastery; just turn up or book ahead.

**Senior Citizens** Mallorca is an excellent destination for older travellers, especially in winter when the resorts are quieter, prices more reasonable and hotels offer very economical long-stay rates. The best deals are available through tour operators who specialise in holidays for senior citizens.

## DRIVING

Speed limits on motorways (*autopistas*): 120kph

Speed limits on main roads: 100kph
Speed limits on minor roads: 90kph

Speed limits on urban roads: 60kph

Seat belts must be worn in front seats at all times and in rear seats where fitted.

Random breath-testing. Limit: 50 micrograms of alcohol in 100ml of breath.

All hire cars take either unleaded petrol (*sin plomo*) or diesel (*gasoleo*). The top grade is *Super Plus* (98-octane), though *Super* (96-octane) is usually acceptable. Petrol stations are normally open 6AM–10PM, and closed Sundays, though larger ones (often self service) are open 24 hours. Most take credit cards. There are few petrol stations in the mountain areas.

If you break down driving your own car and are a member of an AIT-affiliated motoring club, you can call the Real Automóvil Club de España (☎ 971 593 3333). If the car is hired follow the instructions given in the documentation; most of the international rental firms provide a rescue service.

## PHOTOGRAPHY

**What to photograph**: mountains, hilltop monasteries, pretty villages and attractive harbours.
**Best time to photograph**: the Mallorcan summer sun can be powerful at the height of the day making photos taken at this time appear 'flat'; it is best to photograph in the early morning or late evening.
**Film and camera batteries** are available from shops and *droguerías*.

## PERSONAL SAFETY

The national police force, the Policía Nacional (brown unifoms) keeps law and order in urban areas. Some resorts have their own tourist-friendly Policía Turística. If you need a police station ask for *la comisaría*.

To help prevent crime:

- Do not carry more cash than you need.
- Do not leave valuables on the beach or poolside.
- Beware of pickpockets in markets, tourist sights or crowded places.
- Avoid walking alone in dark alleys at night.

Police assistance:
☎ **112**
from any call box

## TELEPHONES

Most public telephones accept coins, credit cards and telephone cards (*tarjetas telefónicas*), available from post offices, news kiosks and tobacconists. Telephone numbers in Mallorca begin with 971; you must dial all nine digits wherever you are calling from. To call Mallorca from the UK dial 00 34; from the USA dial 011 34. To call the operator dial 002.

### International Dialling Codes
From Mallorca (Spain) to:

| | |
|---|---|
| UK: | 00 44 |
| Germany: | 00 49 |
| USA: | 00 1 |
| Netherlands: | 00 31 |

## POST

**Post Offices**
Post Offices (*correus*) are generally open Mon–Fri, 9AM–2PM, but some are also open in the afternoon and on Saturday morning. The main post office in Palma, at Carrer de Constitució 5, is open Mon–Fri, 8:30–8:30, Sat 9AM–2PM ☎ 902 197197

## HEALTH

### Insurance
Nationals of EU and certain other countries can get medical treatment in Spain with the relevant documentation (Form E111 for Britons), although private medical insurance is still advised and is essential for all other visitors.

### Dental Services
Dental treatment is not usually available free of charge as all dentists practise privately. A list of *dentistas* can be found in the yellow pages of the telephone directory. Dental treatment should be covered by private medical insurance.

### Sun Advice
The sunniest (and hottest) months are July and August with an average of 11 hours of sun a day and daytime temperatures of 29°C. During these months especially you should avoid the midday sun and use a strong sunblock.

### Drugs
Prescription and non-prescription drugs and medicines are available from pharmacies (*farmàcies*), distinguished by a large green cross. Pharmacists are able to dispense many drugs which would be available only on prescription in other countries.

### Safe Water
Tap water is generally safe though it can be heavily chlorinated. Mineral water is cheap to buy and is sold as *con gas* (carbonated) and *sin gas* (still). Drink plenty of water during hot weather.

## LANGUAGE

The language that you hear on the streets is most likely to be Mallorquín, a version of Catalan, which itself shares features with both French and Spanish but sounds nothing like either and is emphatically a language, not a dialect. Catalan and Spanish both have official status on Mallorca, and though Spanish will certainly get you by (it is still the language used by Mallorcans to address strangers), it is useful to know some Catalan, if only to understand all those street signs which are being slowly replaced by signs in Catalan.

| | | | |
|---|---|---|---|
| hotel | hotel | chambermaid | cambrera |
| bed and breakfast | llit i berenar | bath | bany |
| single room | habitació senzilla | shower | dutxa |
| double room | habitació doble | toilet | toaleta |
| one person | una persona | balcony | balcó |
| one night | una nit | key | clau |
| reservation | reservas | lift | ascensor |
| room service | servei d'habitació | sea view | vista al mar |

| | | | |
|---|---|---|---|
| bank | banc | credit card | carta de crèdit |
| exchange office | oficina de canvi | exchange rate | tant per cent |
| post office | correus | commission charge | comissió |
| coin | moneda | cashier | caixer |
| banknote | bitllet de banc | change | camvi |
| cheque | xec | foreign currency | moneda estrangera |
| travellers' cheque | xec de viatge | cheap/expensive | barat(a)/car(a) |

| | | | |
|---|---|---|---|
| café | cafè | starter | primer plat |
| pub/bar | celler | main course | segón plat |
| breakfast | berenar | dessert | postres |
| lunch | dinar | bill | cuenta |
| dinner | sopar | beer | cervesa |
| table | mesa | wine | vi |
| waiter | cambrer | water | aigua |
| waitress | cambrera | coffee | cafè |

| | | | |
|---|---|---|---|
| aeroplane | avió | single ticket | senzill-a |
| airport | aeroport | return ticket | anar i tornar |
| train | tren | non-smoking | no fumar |
| bus | autobús | car | cotxe |
| station | estació | petrol | gasolina |
| boat | vaixell | bus stop | la parada |
| port | port | how do I get to...? | per anar a...? |
| ticket | bitllet | where is...? | on és...? |

| | | | |
|---|---|---|---|
| yes | sí | you're welcome | de res |
| no | no | how are you? | com va? |
| please | per favor | do you speak English? | parla anglès? |
| thank you | gràcies | I don't understand | no ho entenc |
| welcome | de res | how much? | quant es? |
| hello | hola | open | obert |
| goodbye | adéu | closed | tancat |
| good morning | bon dia | today | avui |
| good afternoon | bona tarda | tomorrow | demà |
| goodnight | bona nit | right | a la dreta |
| excuse me | perdoni | left | a l'esquerra |

## REMEMBER

- Contact the airport on the day prior to leaving to ensure the flight details are unchanged.

- If travelling by ferry you must check in no later than the time specified on the ticket.

- Spanish customs officials are usually polite and willing to help.

# Index

# TwinPack
## Mallorca

**Written by** Tony Kelly
**Edited, designed and produced by** AA Publishing
**Maps** © Automobile Association Developments 2000, 2002
**Fold-out map** © Freytag-Berndt u. Artaria KG, 1231 Vienna-Austria, all rights reserved

Published and distributed by AA Publishing, a trading name of Automobile Association
Developments Limited, whose registered office is Millstream, Maidenhead Road, Windsor,
Berkshire, SL4 5GD. Registered number 1878835

© **AUTOMOBILE ASSOCIATION DEVELOPMENTS LIMIKTED 2000, 2002**
First published 2000
Revised second edition Sep 2002

A CIP catalogue record for this book is available from the British Library.

**ISBN 0 7495 3455 9**

Colour separation by Chroma Graphics Overseas (PTE) Ltd, Singapore
Printed and bound by Dai Nippon Printing Co (Hong Kong) Ltd.

**ACKNOWLEDGEMENTS**
All pictures used in this publication are held in the Association's own library (AA PHOTO LIBRARY)
and were taken by Peter Baker with the exception of the following: JAINIE COWHAM back cover
tram; KEN PATERSON front cover (g) rubber ring; 1, 5a, 6, 13b, 17, 19, 21, 23a, 24a, 25a, 26, 27b,
28b, 29a, 29b, 30b, 31b, 33, 34, 35b, 36a, 36b, 37b, 39a, 41b, 42b, 44b, 45a, 47a, 47b, 49a, 54,
55, 59, 60, 61a, 90b; JEAN-FRANÇOIS PIN front cover (f) jet skier; HEATHER RAINBOW 41a; ROY
VICTOR front cover (b) cocktail; WYN VOYSEY front cover bottom fishing net 12a, 48a

**TITLES IN THE TWINPACK SERIES**
• Cyprus • Gran Canaria • Lanzarote & Fuerteventura • Madeira • Mallorca • Malta & Gozo •
• Menorca • Tenerife •